Finding God

In An RV

A Spiritual Journey

By

Pat Duggan

To Sue & Bill,

Go With God!

Pat Duggan

All Cover & Original Artwork by Margaret Copfer.

DEDICATION

This book is dedicated to Barbara Copfer, without whom this journey would not have been possible. I am grateful for your love and guidance, in keeping my focus on God. I offer my heartfelt thanks and gratitude for your support and patience on the road and in my writing of this book.

ACKNOWLEDGEMENTS

To God, for giving me the courage to step outside my comfort zone in a remarkable way. Thank you for accompanying us on our journey; for guiding our path; and for keeping us safe every step along the way.

To Margaret Copfer, whose artwork featured on the cover is based on an original painting, entitled 'A Safe Path.' It has provided inspiration for my life and for our journey as we traveled through the most beautiful parts of God's country. Thank you for sharing this piece and for converting it into a beautiful book cover for me.

To Roger Woodruff, Guaranty, Oregon – he is a man truly sent to us by God. He has answered my endless stream of questions, both large and small. I want to sincerely thank him for his support; guidance; and patience throughout our many months of travel. Knowing he was at the end of a phone, willing to help us whenever we had a problem, is a gift we could never repay. We could not have made this trip without your help, Roger, from the beginning and to this day.

Last but not least, to Dave and Phyllis Johnson without whom this journey would never have started. Dave, you were the catalyst God used to launch us on this incredible adventure and we will be eternally grateful to you. Once we decided to embark on this journey, both of you were wonderful in providing help; guidance; and invaluable tips to ensure that a couple of complete amateurs did not run headlong into disaster. We have carried your advice with us and shared it with many.

INTRODUCTION

Where do you look for God? Most recently, for me, I found God in an RV!

Sometimes we look for God and sometimes He just finds us, but perhaps the one consistency in life is that God seems to appear in the most unlikely places. He is found in the midst of horror and disaster; in a new born baby's cry; in a joyful event; in an eagle soaring on a rising air current; or in the petals of a rose as it opens to greet the morning sun. For my part, I had been searching for a while, but on my terms, not on God's terms, I needed a life-changing jolt out of my comfort zone. Perhaps I should explain.

I was born in England, moved to the States thirty years ago, and thought I was settled for my retirement years, with Barbara in a home overlooking the Pacific Ocean on the beautiful Oregon Coast. My life was steady and settled. My thoughts about travel were very limited, involving only the occasional flight and hotel room. Basically, I was happy just being 'a home body.' I drove a modest car, usually a little over the speed limit, because my focus was always on the destination, not the journey. I had an intense dislike for driving in busy city traffic. All in all, my future was quiet, predictable and many would say, boring. Just the way I wanted it, or at least, I thought so. God it seems had other plans for both me and Barb.

One of our pleasures of life in Newport, was to take a daily walk on the boardwalk by the harbor. Several years ago, on our walk we met a couple, who were full time RVers. They had chosen a lifestyle of traveling around the country, sightseeing, visiting places and staying a while in the towns they liked. Newport was one of their favorite stops and they stayed for a couple of months in the summer, each year. They were a fascinating couple and told interesting stories, but it never crossed my mind that one day I would head down the same road.

In subsequent years, Barb and I looked forward to their arrival in town. They could always be found on the same bench overlooking the harbor around four o'clock in the afternoon. Each year we spent time with them, enjoying their company and hearing about their adventures. On each occasion, it was their story and I had no interest in it becoming ours, until one day. As usual, we were discussing multiple subjects, ranging from European affairs, to investment strategies, to the state of the local fishing season. Then Dave made, what was to become, a life-changing comment. He said, "You know, we came to this lifestyle when I came to the realization, that you spend the first half of your life gathering together stuff, and the second half of your life paying to house that stuff."

I have long maintained that God has a 'two by four' with my name on it and not for the first time in my life, I felt Him smack me on the back of the head with it! After many years of my searching, God got my attention with this simple comment from a friend. On that day, I received the life-changing jolt, which would catapult both Barb and I out of our comfort zone, and into a whole new life.

Later, I talked to Barb and told her that Dave's words had struck a chord with me. The only reason we needed our 2400 square foot home was to house all of 'our stuff.' For a while, she had wanted to move back to Ohio to spend more time with kids and grandkids. I had resisted, in part, because I loved our home in Newport, and in part because I did not like the extremes of cold and hot weather in Ohio. Through Dave's profound words, God had instantly severed my emotional attachment to the house and suddenly, their lifestyle offered a potential solution to all of our logistical issues. If we had an RV, we could spend time in Ohio with children in the spring and fall, then escape during the cold winters and hot summers.

And so, this unlikely journey began. First, we sold our house; gave away some of the furniture; sold some of it; and shipped the important stuff back to Ohio for storage. We did a lot of research to figure out the right RV for our needs. Then we had to address all kinds of logistical issues to be able to live a mobile life. Although we did not recognize it at the time, as I look back and reflect on what we did and the decisions we had to make, it is very clear to me that God was directing us in every step along the way. How do I know this? The answer is simple, neither Barb nor I are smart enough to have done so many things right all by ourselves.

Slowly, in God's time, everything came together. We purchased our new motorhome and moved from a 2400 square foot home and into a 330 square foot RV. A new home for Barb, myself and our three cats. We were now completely outside of our comfort zone and about to embark on a journey unlike anything we had ever imagined. I am sure many of our family and friends thought we were crazy, but even though we had no idea what we were doing, both of us were remarkably calm. This can only be described as God's peace.

This has been a journey far beyond my expectations, not only in what God has shown me on the road, but also in what He has taught me during the quiet times. God has blessed me with multiple, undeniable miracles, while giving me a new, and some may say, radical perspective of what it means to know God. I can only say that through this new understanding, my relationship with God has grown and deepened beyond my wildest expectations.

I hope you will keep an open mind as you join me on this amazing journey, in which we found God in an RV.

CHAPTER ONE

Trust & Patience

Patience has never been one of my virtues. Once I have decided to do something, then it becomes my focus and driving force. My motto is, 'let's just get on with it and make it happen.' Jokingly, I have told people that my most frequent prayer is: 'Lord, teach me patience, and teach me NOW!' Joking or not, I can categorically state that it is not a prayer God has ever chosen to answer.

When I had the revelation from God, that I had been holding on to our home out of a desire to surround myself with our 'stuff,' and my perceived prestige that this 'stuff' projected, I had expected things to change quickly. After all, why would God show me so clearly what He wanted me to do and then just stop me in my tracks.

Barb and I had a seemingly endless number of decisions to make. We had to figure out what type of vehicle we would need for our journey – there were many options, towing a trailer, or a fifth wheel, or driving a motor-home – gas or diesel. If we had a motor-home, how would we get around the places we visited? We would need to tow a vehicle, but do we need a car, a truck or an SUV and what size? As we would be living in the vehicle of our choosing, what would we need to take with us; what did we need to put in storage; what should we sell; what should we give away? The choices and decisions to be made were endless and all of them had to be taken from a position of zero experience and knowledge.

We started our research and quickly determined that a motor home was the right choice for us. We went to RV shows and visited dealerships, and with careful and thorough research we settled on the right make, model and floor plan to suit our needs. We chose a Newmar Canyon Star, Model 3610.

In the midst of all these decisions, of course we had a house to sell. Although the housing market in our area was soft, I fully expected everything to move quickly. I was ready to start our new life and I had no doubt in my mind, that this was God's plan.

In my arrogance, I figured out the appropriate order for moving forward. We would sell the house; order our motor home and rent locally for a couple of months until it was ready; during this time, we would figure out which tow vehicle we needed and buy it. This would also give us time to work out all the logistical issues surrounding what to do with all our stuff. All that was left, was for God to just make it happen. Wrong!

After all the initial preparations, we sat and waited for months, the house did not sell. Although our realtor agreed that it was a unique and desirable property, reasonably priced and in a great location. The people who viewed it, liked it, but there was always something, which stopped them from moving forward. This was becoming a real test of my patience.

The old me, would have experienced irritation and frustration. I would have assumed that the delay was in some way my fault and as such, it was my responsibility to fix it. All of my energy would have been devoted to trying to figure out what I had done wrong, and how to make things happen.

Surprisingly, I just seemed to take it in my stride. I knew God had a plan for us, I could not understand why He was not moving us forward, but I trusted that He would work it out. In order to save myself from turning to negativity and defeat, I turned instead to my Bible and to study. It became apparent, that I was experiencing a time of waiting, rest and prayer – not an uncommon occurrence in the Bible. As I studied, primarily through Andrew Wommack's teaching, my relationship with God deepened and strengthened. This, in itself, was a miracle.

In the past, I had encountered God in miraculous ways, but lacked understanding and the right type of guidance, as a result Satan was able to twist the truth in my mind and steal me away from God. Prior to this current life-changing revelation, I had been trying to find my way back, and really needed time to be able to discern God's presence and recognize His miracles when they presented themselves.

Late one afternoon, Barb came into my office and announced that we could tow a Chevy Malibu. It took me a few moments to adjust my thoughts as the tow vehicle discussion had been shelved for months. I responded that I had no idea what a Chevy Malibu looked like and Barb told me there was one at the Chevy dealership across the street. We went over to take a look and within a few hours found ourselves discussing the price. Chevy was offering special pricing that month, which made it a great deal, but the end of the month was the next day. Within forty-eight hours we drove our new car off the lot. We were not in the habit of giving our cars a name, but for the first time each of us was inspired to name it. Without any discussion, we had a conversation and discovered that both of us came up with the same name, although through different thought processes. And so, our new white Chevy Malibu had a name: Angel.

A few weeks earlier, we received a call from our realtors, they had a client coming into town at the weekend, with the intent of putting an offer on our house. At last, things were moving. Immediately we called our salesman at the RV dealership to find out if they had any motor-homes coming in. He responded, one at the end of March (about four weeks), one at the end of April and a used one driving on the lot now. We were so excited, maybe this timing was for us. We raced to the valley to check it out. The vehicle was immaculate and it felt so right, but we decided to wait until the offer was in our hands. We explained to Roger (our salesman) and reluctantly left, trusting and hoping God would take care of it.

The next day, we received a call from the realtor that the buyers had been delayed and would come the following weekend. Then on Sunday, Roger called to tell us the used RV we wanted had been sold. However, his sales manager was willing to offer us a great deal on the new coach coming in at the end of March. We quickly scheduled another trip to the valley to handle the negotiations face to face. After all, we were only days away from receiving an offer on the house, and surely this new vehicle was God's plan for us, it was time to take a step in faith. Our belief was confirmed, when the price negotiations fell into place. The dealer's final figure was $400 below the maximum price Barb and I had previously decided upon, so we signed the deal. When the RV came in at the end of the month, we would test-drive it, confirm the deal and have thirty days to pay for it and drive it away. Everything seemed to be finally coming together and soon we would be able to begin our journey.

Then our realtors told us the buyers had changed their minds completely, they did not want the house and were not even coming into town. Now what do we do? Now we really needed to trust God to sort things out – we could not buy the RV without selling the house and we had just lost the best, in fact the only, potential deal since we started.

We decided to sit tight and wait, only God could get us out of this and I really believed the coach was the one He had chosen for us. The specifications were just what we had planned to order; the timing had seemed to be right; and the price negotiations were close to perfection.

After a couple of weeks, we told Roger that we had not sold the house, but were not willing to back out of the deal yet. The end of March came and went, but there was no sign of the RV. This was good news for us, because until it arrived at the dealership, the thirty-day clock on the purchase agreement, did not start.

Finally, in April, a couple who had looked at the house months earlier, suddenly reappeared and made an offer. We endured a few tense weeks of negotiations and inspections, but the closing was set for the end of May. When the end of April arrived, there was still no sign of the RV, so it was beginning to look like 'God had pulled it off!'

Towards the end of May, we received news that the motor-home had been cleared for transportation by the manufacturers. It was scheduled to arrive in early June. Some friends insisted that we stay with them after the closing on the house until our coach arrived. As we had both ourselves and three traumatized cats, this was a generous offer, which we gratefully accepted.

We marveled at the way God had brought everything together with such precise timing, but He was not finished yet. Our friends were scheduled to leave for vacation on June 14th and we were expecting to move out on the 6th. However, the RV did not arrive as expected. As the clock continued to tick, all four of us wondered how it was going to work out. God's timing was about as close to the wire as it could get. We had our final walk through the coach on the morning of June 12th, and moved in that afternoon. We unloaded a U-Haul full of boxes, then made a quick trip back to Newport to pick up the cats. We spent our first night in our new home that evening amidst the chaos.

A few days later we ventured out in our new home, just to get in a little driving practice. We had found a large, empty parking lot nearby, and decided to use it to practice reversing into a small space. As we traveled down the road, Barb asked me what we should call our new motor-home. Unlike our discussion in naming our car Angel,

16

I responded without any thought or hesitation. My answer was, for both of us, a clear message from God – Guardian. And so, from that moment onwards, we traveled down the road with our own Guardian Angel.

You may recall at the beginning of this chapter, I shared with you my plan of how I thought the preparations for this journey would come together. I could not have been more wrong. Instead of selling the house, ordering the coach and buying the car while we rented for two months waiting for our new home to arrive. God did exactly the opposite, car first, then motor-home, and finally selling the house. It could not have been more clear, I was not in control, this really had been God's plan all along.

This whole process had been a great lesson in trust and patience. There were long periods of waiting, when nothing happened. Then, things began to move, only to stall out and we were back to waiting. There was a period of time when we had made a financial commitment, with no possibility in our own power of fulfilling our obligation, all we could do was to wait on God, and hope. Although I did not fully understand it at the time, God was teaching me, not only patience but also how to trust in His plan. He made this crystal clear by completely turning my plan around, leaving me with no chance of claiming it as my own.

Beside the lessons in patience, trust and hope, we received an unexpected bonus. We had to spend many months in seemingly a 'hurry up and wait mode.' We could not start down-sizing and disposing of furniture, because we did not know how long we would need everything. Later, when the house finally sold, we had to be out on the day of closing, which created a logistical nightmare. We had to decide what to keep; what to ship; what furniture to give away; what we would need in our new home; and how to move everything out of the house. All of this had to be achieved in a very short period of time. Part of our plan had been to give the spare furniture to Goodwill, which seemed to be a quick and easy solution. Then we discovered that they could no longer take any 'soft' furniture, like couches and beds, due to the risk of bed bugs. We were told it would all have to go in the dumpster.

We were really unhappy about dumping a fair amount of good, serviceable furniture, but could see no other solution. Then God, placed a young couple in our path. They lived their lives loving people and trusting God to take care of them despite the difficulties. As a blended family they had six children, including one girl who had been abandoned by her mother. They had just bought a home for their family and all of our spare furniture, came as a God-send to them. However, God did not stop there, the young man willingly stepped up to help us move everything out of the house, into a storage unit, and subsequently onto a truck for shipment to Ohio. In every way, he was a God-send to us too.

We were delighted to know the furniture would help someone after all. We were equally pleased to have the logistical stress of moving furniture and heavy boxes around, lifted from our shoulders. However, the real blessing came much later, when we realized how God had worked out, not only meeting this couple, but also the timing of the whole event. It became clear that if we had sold the house months earlier, they would not have needed the furniture and a later sale would have been too late for them. When this aspect finally struck us, we were in awe of how God operates in multiple, seemingly unconnected lives and brings all things together with such precise timing. This is even more awesome, when you consider, the vast universe under God's watch and that He both knows and cares about an insignificant speck in an obscure corner of the world.

Many people today do not think God still works miracles, or if He does, they are not for ordinary people. I believe the problem is not with God, it is with us. First, we have to expect miracles, and then we must keep our hearts and minds open to recognize them when they come along. They don't happen with a fanfare of trumpets from heaven, but in the unlikely, unforeseen events of everyday life.

When we first made the decision to embark on this new adventure, we did so in the firm belief that it was God's plan for us. With the long wait to sell the house, we could easily have become disillusioned and decided that we were wrong. Thankfully, we held to our belief and not only learned about patience and trusting in God, but were also blessed to experience the miracles of God. We would soon discover that this was just the beginning. As we settled into our new home on wheels, it quickly became clear that God had chosen to travel with us and it was only the beginning of our journey of miracles.

Nugget of Information:

I learned that God has a plan for each one of us, but we must be willing to participate. Throughout our waiting period, I believed I was in God's hands. I needed to learn patience and trust. God revealed himself at the end by completing the plan His way, not mine, with the added bonus of disposing of our unwanted furniture!

CHAPTER TWO

How Does The Bible Fit?

I have worked through various stages in reading my Bible. I was not raised in a church going household, therefore my only exposure to the Bible as I was growing up, was a weekly Religious Instruction class for a few years at Grammar School in England. I also had a weekly class in Greek Mythology, so the Bible just seemed to be another bunch of stories. As I had no context, at best they represented an historical record, but could just as easily have been 'make-believe.'

In my thirties, I read the Bible again. By this time, I was attending a church and at least knew about Jesus. My Bible study was focused on developing my understanding and knowledge, but more from an academic perspective, than a faith one. Years later, I encountered God in my life in a very real way and my studies became intense and more personal. Unfortunately, I did not really have anyone to help me to understand what I was reading and how it related to my life. In

21

my arrogance, I reached a point where I thought I had 'figured out' God and determined that my studies were complete. I had read that God lived within me and reasoned that this meant I had learned all I needed to know, I could just sit back and God would take care of the rest. However, as I was no longer actively participating in my relationship with God, the devil successfully skewed what I had learned and my budding relationship with God, 'withered on the vine.'

I slowly realized I had lost the tenuous connection I had with God, but without any previous foundation, I had no idea what to do. As a result, I spent the next several years wandering in the wilderness.

I had been searching for a while to re-establish my relationship with God and after trying several churches, a friend introduced me to Andrew Wommack's teaching. I listened to his teachings and read some of his books and slowly began to understand the true value of the Bible. I returned to studying the Bible with fresh eyes.

My wakeup call came when we made the decision to sell our home and travel. I believed strongly that this was the direction God was leading me and each event seemed to be a new step confirming this direction. At the same time, each step held a potential for fear and doubt to overwhelm us, and stop the whole process. As we faced the prospect of embarking on a whole new journey, I knew I needed help. I reasoned that, 'God had gotten me into this, therefore, He would have to keep me on track.'

As far as I know, there is no guide to finding God in an RV, so I had to find my own way. I believed God had set me on this path, now I needed to seek out, and this time find God, by developing a lasting relationship with Him. I was fortunate in that I had known God previously, so I had a foundation on which to build. What I lacked were the building blocks to reach a new level of relationship. My recent studies, through Andrew Wommack, provided a starting point and the impetus I needed.

Although I did not understand it at the time, the long wait to sell the house, was at least in part, to allow time for me to grow in my relationship with God, because I would need to be able to trust in Him when we started our journey.

I committed myself to spend time each day with God. I listened to teachings; read books; prayed; and learned to meditate, although not all at the same time. Each of these activities taught me more about the meaning of a relationship with God. I began to learn more about who God is; what He wants to teach me; where He is; and how to pray. All of my studies were Biblically based and as such I was gaining new insight into the Bible through the many quotes I read and heard.

In time, I found myself drawn to different passages. As I read them, although they were familiar, at the same time I saw new truths with a clarity that took my breath away. Why had I not seen before, what was now so obvious? The Bible was coming alive again.

I had experienced this once before many years ago, after my husband passed away. When he died, I turned to God and experienced His presence in my life in a very real way. As I read the Gospels, particularly John, they seemed to speak directly to me. John

14, to me at the time, explained the whole life and purpose of Jesus in a few simple verses, and became the focus of my Christian life. Unfortunately, I saw no reason to look any further and regretfully, dismissed the rest of the Bible.

This time I recognized the similarities of the past, but not just limited to one passage. My studies had broadened my understanding and now my enlightenment was much more broad based. I could see more clearly than ever before that God was showing me who He is and how much He loves me. When the time came to begin our journey, I knew that 'God would be in the driver's seat.'

Let me try to explain a little more clearly what my new Bible insight taught me in more practical terms, and how it related to our journey. There are many lessons to be learned and they are different for each person. In my case, I have come to understand that the Bible never stops giving. The mistake I made last time was to think I had figured it all out, therefore there was no more to learn and I stopped reading. Now I realize that, just as God is infinite, I will always have more to learn. As my journey progresses my needs, skills and desires will progress and change, therefore the Bible will always have something new to teach me.

Although I had some Biblical insight in the past, I found that God was starting me again from scratch. As such, I needed to learn who I am in Christ and about Grace and Faith.

I had previously figured out that God lived within me as this was my great revelation from John 14. However, as "the eyes of my heart were opened," I began to see more clearly what this meant. When I learned that each of us is made up of three parts – body, mind, and

24

spirit. I began to understand that it is the spiritual part of me that is equipped to have a relationship with God. For the most part, we live acknowledging only a carnal existence, which is driven by the mind and body, relying on the five senses – what we can see, taste, smell, touch, and hear. Until recently, I had no idea there was a spiritual part of me and even less idea of how it might affect who I am.

As I had committed myself to connecting with God, the discovery of my spiritual self and how it can affect who I am and how I live was a huge step in my Christian life. The carnal life, driven by the mind and body, has been corrupted and continues to be influenced by the devil. The challenge was to discover how my spiritual self could prevail over my carnal self. I found that the RV life removed many of the normal everyday distractions, to help me seek the answer.

Later as I looked back, this seems quite simple and logical, but in truth, it was a revelation to me. In all the years I had attended different churches, even different denominations, I had never heard anything like this, and yet it now seems so simple and so obvious. Now, as I read my Bible, verses and passages seem to leap out in confirmation of these truths.

Of course, as I indicated, there was and still is much to learn. My next lesson, was about the terms Grace and Faith. Grace was one of those mysterious words frequently used in religious environments but rarely explained. One did not like to ask its meaning, as there was always a sense that one was supposed to know, at least that was how I felt. I remember as a child, I loved the song Amazing Grace, but always assumed it was about a lady called Grace, I had never associated it with God. In subsequent years, I learned it had a Godly connection but never fully understood its meaning, perhaps there was an assumption it was learned in childhood.

Finally, I learned that Grace is what God does for us, independent of us. As a result of Jesus' sacrifice by His death and resurrection, God has already provided forgiveness of sins, healing, deliverance, joy, and peace. The reason Grace and Faith are linked together is that you cannot experience one without the other. Although Grace is freely given and is already available to everyone, we must exhibit Faith to activate the God given Grace. In other words, Faith appropriates what God has already provided by His Grace.

The revelation that I have a spiritual self, together with the beginning of an understanding of Grace and Faith brought me to a whole new place in my life. I could have a relationship with God by connecting with God through my spiritual self. At the same time, I was not relying on my ability to attract God into my life, by His Grace, He was already here, all I had to do was believe. The key was in changing my thoughts to align with who God is and this is achieved through immersion in the Word of God.

****

Our journey began in Oregon and in only four months, we would travel across the Northern States to Ohio and then down to Florida. Along the way, we saw incredible sights, enjoyed many wonders of nature, and met some amazing people. Each day I was able to spend time with God in my studies, although often this time was limited.

Towards the end of our journey to Florida, I learned about meditation. . I came to an understanding that it did not necessarily mean 'sitting quietly in a room with no distractions, staring at a wall and contemplating.' Interestingly, I discovered that the part of the brain used to worry, is the same part used to meditate, therefore meditation is the opposite of worry. One might call it positive worry. Just as we are capable of worrying at any time, we are capable of meditating all the time. All it takes is the use of the imagination focused on the positive. In fact, one can turn one's attention to God at any time and reflect on a word, a verse, or a passage.

One 'leg' of our journey was a 300 mile drive, most of which was on I-65, and as it turned out, it was raining and drizzling. Clearly, I needed to concentrate on the road in the poor conditions, but at the same time endure a boring highway drive. I decided to stay alert by meditating on the first few lines of Psalm 23 – "The Lord is my shepherd, I shall not want, he makes me lie down in green pastures…" This is probably the most well-known Psalm in the Bible and like most people I knew these few lines by heart, but I had never really thought about what it said.

I started with, 'The Lord is my shepherd.' As I considered the words, it came to me that this is The God of the whole universe and as I thought about it, the vastness was awe-inspiring. Then, I considered the next few words, this Lord was willing to shepherd ME. This was not talking about the people of the country in which I lived; or the town I was passing through; or even a group of family or friends. The Lord was interested in being a shepherd to me as a single individual on this huge planet.

My thoughts continued as I considered what a shepherd does and thought about shepherds in Jesus time – he takes care of his sheep; he feeds his sheep; he finds them shelter; and keeps them safe. At night the shepherd would lock his sheep in a pen and then sleep across the entrance to protect them. I thought about a story Jesus told about the shepherd leaving his flock to go out in search of one lost sheep. When he finds the sheep, he picks it up and carries it on his shoulders to bring him home and once safely home, throws a party in celebration.

In these few words, God spoke to me in my meditation and gave me an incredible gift. He showed me that the God of the whole universe cares about me as an individual. He is my very own shepherd and as such he is taking care of me, feeding me, keeping me safe and prospering me on my journey. The long 300 mile drive was not boring after all as it was spent in communion with God. In addition, the mental activity kept my mind sharp, so that I was able to stay focused on the road and its less than favorable conditions.

About a week later, after we had settled in our home for the winter, the small town of Carrabelle, in Florida, God gave me another unexpected gift. I was walking along the beach by the water's edge and thinking about the beauty of God's creation. About a hundred yards ahead of me, I saw a small boat, just a few yards off the beach and a line of floats from a fishing net stretched across to the shore. There were two or three men in the boat and on the shore. As I looked at this scene, it seemed to come straight out of the Bible. My thoughts turned to Jesus walking beside the Sea of Galilee in Matthew 4:18-20. He comes across Simon Peter and his brother Andrew as they cast a net into the lake. Jesus calls them saying, "Come follow me, and I will make you fishers of men." As I walked towards the group, I wondered if I was seeing what Jesus had seen as he walked along the water's edge, so many years ago.

The experience I have just related was deeply moving at the time. However, as I sit here recalling the details to write it down, I am reminded of the previous occasion I studied this passage and it has taken on even greater significance. I previously indicated that I had studied the Bible at various stages in my life.

The first such occasion was back in England in the mid-seventies. I had become a member of the Methodist Church and had experienced what is referred to as 'a call to preach.' The Methodist Church in England could not afford a minister for each church, therefore many times a lay-person, known as a 'local preacher' would preach on Sunday. If a person felt God was calling them to preach, it was necessary to stand before the Local Preachers in the circuit and explain their call. If the group believed the call was genuine, the individual embarked on a comprehensive training program. Becoming a Methodist Local Preacher involved a two-year correspondence course, while accompanying and assisting an experienced local preacher throughout this period.

I had undergone the required training and my final test, involved preaching my first sermon. I chose as my text Matthew 4:18-20 – 'I will make you fishers of men.' I had not thought about this passage for many years and am once again in awe that on a beach in Florida, many years and many thousands of miles later, God gave me the gift of actually seeing what Jesus saw, when He spoke those words.

Nugget of Information:

God is always seeking a relationship with us and will continue to work with us as long as we are looking for Him. All the answers are to be found in the Bible, if we prayerfully look for them. Meditating on a verse or a passage, can help you to find the answers. The Bible teaches us what God has already given to us by Grace. However, it is our Faith which activates God's Grace.

CHAPTER THREE

What Is It Saying About Me?

I sat down this morning to read my Bible, but first, I asked God to 'open the eyes of my heart' and let me see what He wanted to teach me. God said to me, "What is it saying about Me?"

This gave me a whole new perspective to what I was reading. I have, in the past, read the Bible, particularly the New Testament, almost as an historical document, which tells the story of the life of Jesus and who He was. I have read the accounts of Jesus life and tried to put myself there to be a part of what was happening, and consider how it would have affected me to be in that place. I have read passages trying to discern what God was trying to show me or teach me at that moment. However, I had not spent time thinking about who God is and how the Bible provides me with a window to see God.

I am English and as such, the only perspective I have about 'King,' comes from a lifetime of watching the royal family and learning about their history. In a sense this was my only point of reference, so I used to think about God as a king sitting on a throne, in some distant place, called heaven. In my mind, He was inaccessible to mere mortals. I have now come to a place in which my understanding has radically changed. I believe God is waiting for me to 'open the door to His castle.' He wants to have a relationship with me, but I must make the first move. God is not far away, as I had previously imagined, He is as close as I want Him to be.

My first step was to recognize that God is a spirit. Of course, I know this intellectually, however, if I rely only on my intellect, He remains inaccessible. My challenge was in changing my understanding. As I grew in knowledge, I accepted myself as one-third spirit. As a spiritual person as well as a carnal person, I can relate to and communicate in the spirit realm. God is a spirit dwelling in the spirit realm, and I am, in part, spirit, therefore God is no longer inaccessible in a distant place. I can commune with God. In order to do so, I must find a way to know God.

All healthy relationships develop and flourish through a process of getting to know each other. God as my creator already knows every atom of my being. It is my task and challenge in life to know God. The only tangible link I have to God is the Bible. It is only through God's Word that I can develop my knowledge of God, which, I believe is the key to having a relationship with God.

In many ways, I think today's society has lost its connection with words. Of course, we must still communicate, but this is done in a

32

much abbreviated form with texts, tweets and such like. The importance of words has largely been lost. As a result, the action of reading primarily involves scanning the page to pick up 'the gist of the story.'

Thankfully, I have not succumbed to the new standard of communicating with acronyms and indeed I struggle when called upon to do so. Although I still prefer to read complete sentences, even I did not fully appreciate the true value of words until recently. In my studies I have read and heard many Biblical references about words. For example, Prov. 18:21 - "Death and life are in the power of the tongue," and Rom. 10:17 – "Faith comes by hearing, and hearing by the Word of God."

As I began to appreciate the value of words, the obvious reference jumped out at me. All of us know it, but if you are like me, you don't really hear it for what it is actually saying. John 1:1 – "In the beginning was the Word, and the Word was with God, and the Word was God." The awesome power of God is such that all He needs to do is to speak and it is so.

This led me to the understanding that if words are important as I study the Bible, then it is necessary to pay attention to all of them. After all, the inescapable message of John 1:1 is that God is to be found in the Word. I believe this is not just the collective Word of God, which is the Bible, but also in the detail.

As I put this to the test, and took time to read each word, I saw details I had not seen before, even in passages I thought I knew. All of us are familiar with Jesus commandments in Mk. 12:30-31 – "Love the Lord your God with all your heart and with all your soul and with all your mind and with all your strength. The second is this: Love your neighbor as yourself." Most of us simplify this to 'we are called to love God and our neighbor,' I know, I did. However, when I focused on the detail, I realized, God also calls us to 'love self.' In other words, we are called to 'love God, <u>self</u>, and others.'

This gives the passage an important balance, which is often missed. On the one hand, if we don't love self, we are incapable of loving someone else. Unfortunately, in today's society, self-centeredness has become the norm, as many people think only about themselves, which was not God's plan for us. On the other hand, the religious focus is often exclusively on loving one's neighbor, which imposes 'a law' that is impossible to keep. If we give all of Jesus' words equal value, we can find that balance, and as a result, with God's help a greater purpose in our lives.

A word of caution is necessary at this point, as it is easy to become so involved in one's own understanding in studying he Word of God. Such study cannot be purely an intellectual activity, it is absolutely vital that it remains a spirit activity. In other words, all studies of the Word of God must be guided by the Holy Spirit within us. In this matter, I speak from experience, in that at one time in my life I studied the Bible and allowed my intellect to take over. This opened a door for Satan to take hold of the Word and twist its meaning such that my ego overwhelmed me. It took a while for me to realize my error and even longer for me to find my way back into relationship with God,

As a result of this 'wandering in the desert' experience, I always pray for God's guidance in my studies. Nonetheless, I have found myself changing my focus as I read the Bible, to a perspective of 'what it is telling me about God,' as I believe this will bring me closer to Him. Of course the Old Testament is focused on God and often portrays a vengeful and wrathful God. On the other hand, the New Testament focus, particularly the gospels, is primarily on Jesus.

Recently, I was reading the Gospel of John, which is still my favorite Gospel, and I have read it many times. I came to John 15, and in the past I have looked at this just from the perspective of Jesus as the 'vine' and me as a 'branch,' hopefully being pruned to bear fruit. On this occasion, I was looking for God and was surprised to find that He played such a prominent role in this passage. Verse one reads, "I am the true vine, and my Father is the gardener." It continues in verse two with, "He cuts off every branch in me that bears no fruit, while every branch that does bear fruit, He prunes so that it will be even more fruitful." Although I am a gardener myself, I had never considered that Jesus needed a gardener, let alone that God was the gardener. This revelation gave me a whole new perspective to a passage I thought I knew.

Clearly, with God's guidance, studying the Word in the light of 'what is it saying about me?' provides for a new level of understanding. It never ceases to amaze me that one can read a passage over and over, and yet it yields new information and insight, just when God needs to show us something different.

This is equally true of all aspects of our life, if we remain open to hearing God's prompting. In our travels, I seem to have been particularly attuned to God's prompting. On many occasions as we traveled across the country, we have responded to God prompting us to take a certain route or travel to a certain campground or to stay an extra day in a specific location. In all of our travels, we have always had a strong sense that God was taking care of us. Our route, the timing and our stops in hindsight have often revealed a purpose, sometimes the reason remains a mystery to us although we know it is in God's hands.

One experience of God working out His plan was when we were at Newmar. We had been scheduled to leave on the Wednesday, but outside contractors had not completed their work and we were delayed. We were in the service department's parking lot when a gentleman walked past our car. I turned to Barb and said he looked familiar, but not someone we had met recently. She said he looked like a person we had met while staying at the Elks in Newport more than two months earlier, but the likelihood of seeing him here in Nappanee, Indiana seemed virtually impossible. As unlikely as it seemed, I had to know and I went after him. As I followed him across the parking lot, calling his name, his wife stepped out from behind her car. She had purchased a supplement from us, while in Newport and I had called her several times to follow up with her, but without success. As soon as she saw me, she quickly explained that she had stopped taking it as it had upset her system. Since then, she had not called because she was now in considerable abdominal pain and she just wanted to get home and see her doctor. They had arrived at Newmar that morning, having traveled down from Canada, to have a slide-out adjusted, before continuing home to Arizona. Later in the day we talked and I suggested taking our Aloe Juice supplement, as it might give her some relief for the rest of the journey home, and it certainly would not do any harm. The next day we left, but received a call three days later to say she was much better and the pain was almost gone. God had put together numerous different pieces, involving multiple people to work out His plan and all of it was outside the control of any of us.

While we were in Nappanee, I did experience God's prompting one morning and thankfully acted on it. I woke up with the sense that the bare wall at Barb's side of the bed, needed a picture. Later, we were wandering through an old factory, which had been converted to stores, and came across a Christian bookstore. There were pictures on the walls and Barb drew my attention to one with an eagle flying over snow covered mountains and the quote from Isaiah 40:31. I had not mentioned my 'morning revelation' to Barb, but she knows my passion for eagles and their spiritual majesty. I loved the picture, but it was outside of our budget. I asked if they had a smaller copy or could offer any discount and the assistant promised to check with the owner and call me. I turned it over to God and trusted that He would work it out if it was supposed to be on the wall. The next morning, Jolleen from the store called and told me there were several other pictures using the same passage or she could give me a coupon for 20% discount. We returned to the store and although there were several other options, they did not have the eagle picture. Even with the discount, the picture was a little more than I had hoped to pay, but I trusted that I was following God's prompting and we bought the picture. Later, we received the bill for the work on the coach, I noticed that the cost of the oil change was much higher than the quote I had received. By the time the price adjustment had been made, the saving more than covered the cost of our new picture. I had followed God's prompting from waking up the previous morning and through the next day. At each step I moved forward as I believed God was leading me and He worked everything out without us 'busting our budget.'

As our journey continued, I tried to study and read my Bible each day and develop my relationship with God. Our travels brought us to

Carrabelle, Florida and after a long and tiring drive we reached the campground and were directed to our spot. This was to be our new home for the next three months. As I pulled into the space, I experienced a powerful dis-ease and actually refused Barb's prompting to pull too far forward. The front window looked out over a large drainage pit, although it had no water and I fully understood its purpose, I was not comfortable.

The next morning, before Barb woke up, I talked to God. Did He really want us in this spot? Or should we be somewhere else? I was concerned about not trusting God to have brought us to the right place. Perhaps the devil was messing with me. My most recent studies through Andrew Wommack, had shown me that one way to determine God's direction for me was to weigh up all the options and the right one would be accompanied by God's peace.

When Barb woke up, we discussed the options and as I was still ill at ease with the current location, we decided that God would provide a new location, if we were supposed to move. We stopped at the office and spoke to Jenn. She told us the current location was the only one available for our three-month stay, particularly as there was a major event in the resort coming up that weekend. She would check to see if we could move the next week but it would probably mean changing sites several times. We took a walk to discuss it, then came back and asked her to start checking, even if it meant multiple moves. She started her search and immediately found a spot available from the following Monday until the end of our stay. She gave us the site number and we went to check it out. It only took a few minutes to decide it would work. The next week we moved into our new location and immediately settled into God's peace.

These experiences hopefully demonstrate how God can guide your life, if you are open to it and follow faithfully. In order to recognize God's prompting, it is necessary to spend time reading and studying the Word. Words in all instances matter, but the Word of God is our life's blood. Reading the Bible can be read superficially, but it's real value is found when it is read with the guidance of the Holy Spirit instead of relying on one's intellect. In doing so, I found that I received an added gift when I read the New testament looking for God's part in the story, instead of just assuming it was only about Jesus.

Nugget of Information:

Reading the Bible, with a focus on 'What is it Saying About God,' highlights the importance of words. Only when you consider and put equal value on each word, does the true meaning of a passage come to light. Remember: John 1:1 – "In the beginning was the Word.

CHAPTER FOUR

Meeting God Where He Is

One of the major challenges in my walk with God through the years, has been - Where is He?

I have attended churches; embraced music ranging from traditional hymns to contemporary spiritual music; read my Bible; and of course, I have prayed. Each of these activities have been my attempts to 'bring God to me.' I always assumed that my relationship with God somehow involved my ability to attract Him into my world. Recently, God has shown me that the opposite is true, developing a relationship with Him, is to meet God in His world.

Let me try to explain. I live in the physical world we all know. It is one in which we depend on our five senses to function. Everything in this world revolves around what we can see, taste, touch, hear, and smell. My concept of God, used to be based on these limitations and as such, my only hope for knowing Him was to resort to my emotions to feel His presence.

Several years ago, I had an encounter with God in which I felt the love of God wash over me as I prayed. It was a very real, almost tangible, experience at a time in my life when I needed to know I was loved. My husband of twenty-three years, had just passed away. He had been the love of my life and I was facing the rest of my life alone, without any expectation of having anyone to love me again. I had no intention of risking my heart a second time, as the pain of loss was too great. Although I had been an active Christian in the past, at this time I had not attended church or turned to God in prayer for many years. I lived wholly in the physical world I knew. It was in this desperate state that God met me in my world and gave me the wonderful gift of directly experiencing His love. It was a miracle and I will always feel blessed to have known such love on a personal and intimate basis.

Unfortunately, I did not understand that my encounter with God was a gift for the moment and not a state for my life. As a result, I spent a lot of time trying to recapture the moment again. I assumed that in some way I had failed and it was up to me to do something to 'bring God back.' After all, I had experienced God in my world and this was the only world I knew.

I knew the Bible told me that God was a spirit, but my lack of knowledge and understanding prevented me from seeing the possibility of an accessible world beyond the one I knew. I had never given the whole idea much thought, but had I been asked, I guess, I perceived Heaven as a distant world, hopefully to become known to me, after death. In my mind, God as a spirit was free to travel 'down' to earth, and might choose to make himself known to individuals on occasion. It had never occurred to me to question this concept and I had not heard any teaching to provide a different explanation. In fact, any reference to a 'spirit realm' came to me with negative connotations, associated more with fairground fortune-telling than with God. As such, there was nothing good about it and it was a subject to avoid.

Recently in my Biblical studies, God has shown me that He lives in the spirit realm, which is actually more real than the physical realm. More importantly, through the Holy Spirit within me, I can connect with the spirit realm and as such develop my relationship with God, in His world. The Bible teaches that the physical world was God's creation, therefore it stands to reason that the spirit realm existed first.

When I began to wrap my mind around the concept of God abiding in the spirit realm, which exists in parallel with our world, instead of somewhere beyond the universe, important factors seemed to fall into place. If I have access to the spirit world, then it would seem much easier for me to seek God in His world, rather than to try to 'make' Him come to my world.

I have accepted the Lord and become a 'born again' Christian, and have experienced the baptism of the Holy Spirit. I believe the Holy Spirit lives within me and as such, I know the spirit part of me is clean and pure. I understand that as God is spirit, He must be spiritually discerned. It is the spiritual part of me that connects with God and receives insight and discernment. As Rom. 8:6 states; 'To be carnally minded is death, to be spiritually minded is life and peace.' As my search for a closer relationship with God continued, I came to realize that the Christian Life is an exchanged life. It is living in the spirit, instead of living in the physical or carnal world.

Of course, I still live and breath in this physical world but I am learning to rely more on God by 'tapping into' the spirit world. It is the spiritual part of me, which turns to God and in a sense, hands over control of my life. I say 'hands over control,' but in truth I never had control anyway, which makes my life much easier. I came to a place where I finally understood that I was powerless to make things happen, at that point trusting God became much easier. Our journey in the RV has become an ongoing demonstration of meeting God where He is and just trusting that He will take care of us, no matter what the circumstances may be.

The decision to set out on a new journey and live fulltime in an RV was a huge step. I have always owned a 'brick and mortar' home and was raised to believe this represented security. I have always had a support system around me, whether it was family or friends, if I needed help. Of course, the biggest step out of my comfort zone, was that I have never driven anything larger than a Ford Windstar and had never even been camping.

Selling our house, buying an RV and setting out on the open road, without any firm plan about where we were going, and even less idea of how we would get there, was to some of our family and friends the action of crazy people. However, from our perspective, it was an act of faith. We had nobody to help us, and nobody to rely on, apart from God.

As it has turned out, God is all we need and He has shown us that truth, time and time again. After buying the coach, we stayed on the

44

dealership lot for a week or so. We had a tremendous learning curve to overcome, even before setting off down the road. If you think about it, a motor-home holds all the complexity of a house, with all its systems, furniture and fixtures together with the biggest vehicle you have ever owned. All of these moving parts have to operate in sync with each other as the whole thing bounces down the road.

We had to figure out basic things like, what we needed, from teaspoons to a barbeque grill and washcloths to blankets, plus clothes for whatever season we may encounter. Then we had to pack them all into a few hundred square feet, instead of spreading out into the 2400 square feet we previously lived in. Next, we had to figure out how the heating and cooling system worked; how to get water and electric; the finer points of dealing with our own waste; as well as cooking and cleaning.

The first big test came when we left the relative security of the dealership and headed back to Newport to tie up the loose-ends surrounding our move. I knew we had to drive across the Coast Range on a road which is not really recommended for RVs and being afraid was not going to make the journey any easier. I needed to approach this trip with confidence or this big investment and wild plan, was not going to work. As I pulled off the lot and headed down the road, I reasoned that God had gotten us into this situation, so He was going to have to help me out. Silently, I took a deep breath and handed the steering wheel over to God. As a result, I instantly became calm, even through the heavy rain we soon encountered, and on the narrow, winding road of the Coast Range. From that day forward, every time I get behind the wheel, I turn it over to God. Of course, I hold onto it and turn it as necessary, but I am trusting God for our safety and I know inwardly that I could not do this without

God's help. After more than five thousand miles at this point, it has become a moment-by-moment confirmation that this is where we are supposed to be.

After our stay in Newport, we returned to the familiarity of the dealership lot for them to address a few problems discovered on our first trip. All new rigs have 'teething problems' and we had expected to spend time getting them fixed before we began our journey.

Finally, it was time to venture out and break new ground. We decided to make our first trip a relatively short one and planned to stop at the Keizer Elks Club, close to Portland. As we were new to this lifestyle, it seemed prudent to plan where we would be staying ahead of time, rather than driving and hoping to find somewhere when we were ready to stop. The downside with the Elks Club, was that they do not take reservations, it is strictly first come, first served. When we called the night before to check on availability, we were told they had three spots and we reasoned that if we started at a reasonable time, we would arrive early enough to secure a spot.

However, the next morning it soon became clear that we would have to rely on God for our spot, instead of my planning and reasoning. Our departure from the dealership was delayed and then we encountered further delays on the road due to a traffic accident. It did occur to us that we may have been part of the accident if we had left when we had intended to leave, and perhaps God had protected us from disaster. As time slipped by, we knew the limited spots available at the Elks, may well be taken. All we could do, was pray that God would ensure there was space for us, if not, we had nowhere to stay for the night. Not for the first time, we placed ourselves in God's hands and trusted He would take care of us. We arrived at the

Elks, and as we drove in, saw one spot directly in front of us, apparently just waiting for us. As we unhooked the car, someone came over and confirmed we could take this last available pull-through. As I had little experience of backing into a parking space with this 37 foot rig, I was relieved to have an easy way in and out. Once we were settled, we found there was only one other spot left, a back-in, and that was quickly filled. God had taken care of us on our first venture away from our comfort zone.

We had owned our new home for several weeks and made short trips within Oregon, including a trip to see friends in Medford. Although we felt adventurous, in reality, we were close enough to friends that we still had a safety net. The time arrived, when we had to venture out of our comfort zone. We were leaving the state; our friends; and our support group and now our reliance would be on God for all things – help, guidance, support, and friend. The experiences of God guiding us and supporting us in all we had done so far, served to strengthen our relationship with God and our faith that He would be with us in our journey.

We left Portland and the first test came as we drove through the magnificent Columbia River Gorge. As always, I had begun the trip by turning over the steering wheel to God. This was just as well, as soon we encountered strong and unexpected cross-winds. It was a little unnerving to feel the motor-home moving sideways, without me turning the steering wheel, and it took a few moments for me to understand what was happening. Thankfully, God kept us safe as there was nobody on the roadway, and He corrected our course and steered us safely down the road. I quickly learned to mitigate the effect of the wind by slowing down. My actions and reactions were not from being taught what to do, they came through an intuitive knowledge which can only be explained through my connection with the God-given spiritual realm.

Our next encounter with difficult road conditions came as we drove across South Dakota, several weeks later. I had now become more comfortable with driving our home on wheels, but still turned the steering wheel over to God each time we set out. On this day, we endured crosswinds, with the added challenge of road works involving fast moving traffic in close quarters. The buffeting and crosswinds were relentless and continued for miles. Then we encountered the added challenge of rain as we passed through Iowa. These conditions continued for hours, and I know God kept us on course because the physical effort would have been too much for me to handle through my own strength. Thankfully, we arrived safely at our destination in Joliet, Illinois.

God's guidance on our journey was not limited to keeping us on the road through bad weather and poor road conditions. We relied on Him through every aspect of our journey, and discovered that God was a master navigator.

As our journey continued, we continued to encounter God in our travels. He meets us unexpectedly to show us the way. Often our need only comes to light after the fact, in that we look back and see how He protected us and kept us on course.

On one such occasion we had been in Nappanee, Indiana at the Newmar factory, before heading south to spend the winter months' out of the cold weather. Our route would take us through Indianapolis, the prospect of navigating round a big city was a little daunting, but we had Grace, our GPS system. It seems like everyone names their GPS, we had chosen Grace.

Anyway, we programmed Grace for our destination which was Scottsburg, Indiana and set out. We approached Indianapolis around noon, when the traffic was still relatively light. It was clear that there were major road works on the road around the city involving lane changes and diversions, which were not fully covered by Grace. She initially led us on one diversion, but it quickly became clear that it was more extensive than our GPS was aware. Thankfully, we made it through the first diversion without any problem. However, an even more complex road change followed. Once again, God was there to meet us and guide the way. Grace led us through the first turn off, but more options quickly followed and Grace had no instruction to offer. On the GPS screen, she quickly deposited the coach in a field! We had no idea which direction to take, but God had directed me to review the map before we left, even though this was not my usual practice, and from that recollection, I had a sense we needed to keep West. We were traveling on a major highway with no space to pull over due to the construction all around us, decisions had to be made in seconds, I followed my God-given sense of direction and prayed it would be correct. God's prompting led us 'out of the field,' and onto the right road. Grace quickly recalculated and our journey resumed. In due course, we arrived safely at Jellystone Campground, in Scottsburg.

I have related just a few of the ways God has accompanied us on our journey across the country and kept us safe, even in adversity. They provide clear evidence of God's Grace, accompanied by our Faith. This faith is the result of a deepening relationship with God as

I continue to learn to spend time in the spiritual realm and tap into the intuition that comes only through knowledge of God.

Nugget of Information:

God is a spirit and lives in the spirit realm. Through the work of the Holy Spirit, I am one third spirit. As a result, I can connect with God through the spiritual part of myself and meet God in His world, instead of trying to make Him come into my world.

CHAPTER FIVE

Go With God

A phrase that rolls off the tongues of many Christians, is 'Go With God,' but have you ever given these words any thought or consideration. If you are like me, it is just something spoken and received as a casual statement of kindness. What if we were to take it literally?

God created us for a purpose and I believe this purpose was to be in fellowship with Him. When God created Adam and Eve, He breathed life-giving spirit into them. They had a spiritual part to them, which was pure and the story spoke of God walking in the garden to commune with them in the evening. When they ate from the tree of knowledge, they became sinful, lost their purity, and were banished from the Garden of Eden. I am sure we all know the story from childhood.

51

Until recently, I had assumed that God was angry with Adam and Eve and leaving the Garden of Eden also meant leaving the presence of God. However, when I read Gen. 3:22 carefully, my long held assumption was clearly wrong. God banished Adam and Eve from the Garden of Eden, not out of anger, but to save them from eating from the Tree of Life. This would have resulted in them living forever in there sinful state, surely death would be preferable. In the following verses, it also becomes clear that God continued to have a relationship with them as we read that the Lord gave Eve a son, Cain.

Clearly God maintained a relationship with Adam and Eve, even in their sinful state, therefore it seems reasonable to conclude it is His wish to be in relationship with all his people. This is borne out in the Old Testament, as the kings and prophets each had a relationship with God, which continued even when they sinned and failed to follow His will.

I believe this is still true today. God desires to be in relationship with His people. Unfortunately, this concept seems to have become lost in religious dogma and the increasing prevalence of self-centeredness amongst society in general.

Relationship is a two-way street. It is not about paying lip service through attending a brief worship service, one day a week, or even about nightly prayer, in which we tell God what we did wrong (Newsflash: He already knows). I believe God wants us to commit to Him and share our life with Him – but how?

As we journeyed across the country, I was learning that 'Finding God' was not about bringing God into my world, but through the spiritual part of me, it was meeting God in His world.

Most of us accept God is a spirit, but we seek God by trying to pull Him into our physical world. It makes more sense for us to join Him in His world. The first step is to recognize that there is a spiritual world, which is already here and is all around us. As I have already indicated, each one of us consists of three parts, spirit, soul and body, not just the two parts (soul and body) we normally live by. As born again Christians, our spiritual self has been renewed through Christ and is one hundred percent pure. As such, our spiritual self can, and I submit, should approach God in His world.

Once I accepted this truth, and understood I am one third spiritual self, I wanted to know more. I learned * that I had been living a carnal, sinful life, in which my body was driven by my mind, which relied only on the five senses. When I brought the spiritual part of myself into the equation, I had a sense of wanting to change. However, my analytical mind, showed me that I was fighting a losing battle, just wanting my spiritual self to prevail was not enough. My carnal self was under the control of my mind and body, and this could not be overcome by a wishful spiritual self, it was simply two against one. There had to be a solution.

It soon became apparent that as my physical body was controlled by my mind through my thoughts, the answer was to change my thoughts. The only way in which this 'balance of power' can change, is for my spiritual self to affect my carnal self. I came to understand that it is our thoughts, which drive the body and make us who we are. Therefore, if I could change my thoughts and bring them in-line with my spiritual self, I would become closer to God. I found that spending time reading and studying the Word of God was the 'window' into my thoughts and the way to refocus my mind. A

53

refocused mind leads to new thoughts, perspectives and priorities, and these begin to move the body in a different direction. I found confirmation of this theory in verses like Prov. 23:7 - "As he thinks in his heart, so is he." Rom. 10:17 – "Faith comes by hearing, and hearing by the Word of God."

In fact, the more I read, the more passages I found to confirm this simple truth, and yet, I had never noticed it before. It is one of the miracles of the Bible that you can read it over and over and not see the message it holds, until the Spirit within us opens our mind to the truth. As it says in Eph. 1:17-18 – "that God may give you the Spirit of wisdom and revelation in the knowledge of him, having the eyes of your heart enlightened, that you may know what is the hope to which he has called you…"

As I began to read my Bible, with renewed eyes, I have begun to change my thoughts. Although I realize this is a lifelong task, as I continue in this way, my mind is becoming more in line with my spirit and 'the balance of power' is changing. As my mind and spirit are coming into alignment, they overcome my carnal self and my body follows the new spiritual rule.

I have reached a place where I am beginning to experience this change in some instances, although sadly I still revert back to my carnal self. However, I now see the possibilities and know that as I continue to renew my mind, I will become more attuned to my spiritual self and therefore grow into a closer relationship with God.

After we started our journey eastward, I experienced a demonstration of this change in the balance of power in my life and how God, literally redirected our path to meet His purpose.

Shortly after leaving Oregon, we received an email telling us that my mentor on this journey to find God, would be speaking in Portland, Oregon the following weekend. I was really disappointed, as we were already out of the state and unable to return. As a solutions driven person, I reverted to my carnal self, to figure out the answer. I checked online to determine where Andrew Wommack was due to speak in the coming months, certain that God would have arranged for our paths to cross. When I noted he would be in Chicago, I thought this was the answer, but our planned schedule made it impossible to get there in time. I resigned myself to the fact that it was not time yet and God would work it out for later in the year, either in Florida or Texas, and I let it go.

A little later, we were in Polson, Montana and had plans to visit Yellowstone and then Mount Rushmore. Our journey would take us across the country through the summer, with the intent of arriving in Ohio for the fall to visit family and see our grandson play soccer. While in Polson, I woke up one morning with an overwhelming feeling that if we kept to our current schedule, we would not be back in Ohio in time for soccer. I shared this concern with Barb and we sat down to plan out the journey in detail.

We had a map marked with campsites and figured out each step, calculating the mileage between the stops. We still wanted to visit Yellowstone and Mount Rushmore, but Barb suggested reducing the time we had planned to stay at each location. I made a note of each stop, the number of miles, and the length of our stay, to ensure we could reach Ohio in the first part of September.

We discovered that the most direct route would take us south of Chicago and one of the intended stops would be at Joliet, Illinois. This area had few campgrounds marked on the map and our planning was based on the mileage from one RV park to the next.

When we had calculated and listed each stop, from Montana to Ohio, my thoughts returned to the Wommack Conference. I counted the number of days on our schedule to the date we would arrive in Joliet and literally stopped in stunned silence. The new schedule put us in Joliet on the day Andrew Wommack arrived in Chicago, and he was scheduled to speak the following morning.

I turned to Barb and said, "I didn't plan it, honestly!" She laughed and responded, "I know, I was the one who decided how many days we should stay at Yellowstone and at Mount Rushmore."

There was no explanation for this chain of events, other than divine influence. Although I believed that I was to attend a Wommack Conference at some point, and I had tried to make it happen, I had resigned myself to an assumption the timing was not right and had dismissed it for the present. In hindsight, I believe God woke me up and led both of us to review and change our travel plans. It was clearly impossible for us to just map out a 2,300 mile trip over a three week period and have it work out to the day without any pre-planning. And yet, this is how it came together, it was truly a miracle.

We had no doubt God was calling us to attend the Conference, and without hesitation, immediately booked the tickets online. During the long journey that followed, God blessed us over and over again as you will see from the events documented in these pages. We had occasional challenges along the way, with weather issues, and even a GPS malfunction but God stepped in and kept us on schedule.

On the last day of our journey, we had programmed the RV Park into our GPS and approached Joliet at the end of a long day's drive. As we took an off ramp from the interstate, Grace, our GPS, told us we had reached our destination. Although we could see a Campground below us, there was no access to it from the interstate. The ramp took us onto another interstate and we had no option but to keep driving down the road. As Barb scrambled to find our backup written directions, she recognized the information on the next exit and we instinctively took it. Still trying to figure out where to go next, Barb recognized the street name ahead of us, as the one for the campground and once again we turned onto it. There was no sign for the RV Park and after a mile or so, we had serious doubts about the direction we were taking. I pulled over to allow a car to pass us and to our amazement, the driver put his arm out of the driver's window and signaled that we should follow. About a mile further down the road was a sign to the campground, just before our 'good Samaritan' driver turned off the road. A few minutes later, we reached our destination.

From the time we left Oregon and even before, I took at least a few minutes each day to talk to God. Most days, I spent time in study to relearn the things I thought I knew, about how to communicate with God. For instance, prayer is not about reading a long list of requests and pleas to get God to give me what I need. In truth, God not only knows what we need, He has already provided it. Prayer is primarily about thanking God for what He has done, whether we can see it yet or not and about praising Him for who He is. There were many words of thanks on the day we arrived in Joliet.

In this whole journey, we have not known what we needed and just trusted God for our safety. In my studies, I wanted to know more about God and learn as much as possible, but throughout this time, my underlying aim was, is and always has been to grow in my relationship with God. We just wanted to follow wherever God led us – to Go With God!

Nugget of Information:

One third of me is spirit but my carnal self is controlled by my mind and body. The key is to change my thinking through study of the Word. As my mind is changed, my body must follow as the two to one equation applies; the majority rules, and I am moved into a spirit driven life.

*Spirit, Soul and Body by Andrew Wommack

CHAPTER SIX

God & The Animals

At this point I have shared with you some of the revelations I have received from God about developing a relationship with Him. However, this journey has not been 'all work.' God has introduced us to His world of the animals in an amazing and unexpected way.

One of our early sightseeing stops was Polson, Montana. Our plan was to visit Glacier National Park, but this area had so much more to offer. We quickly discovered the National Bison Range was located only a few miles away from the campground. When we started our journey and left Oregon, I told Barb, I had never seen a bison and really hoped we would see one on our journey.

The realization that the bison range was close-by, seemed to be my chance to fulfill a dream. We learned that the park had much more to offer than just bison, when we stopped at the ranger's station. We received a map of the two main routes through the park and were advised to take our time and observe. We chose the long loop and set off. I briefly saw a bison in the distance and towards the end of the loop we could see a herd some way off but in terms of bison spotting it was a little disappointing.

However, on that day, God had other gifts in mind for us. We drove slowly and allowed several vehicles to pass us as we kept a keen eye out for anything that moved. We reached a quiet stretch of road and spotted movement ahead just a few yards off the road in some shrubs. When we got closer, we realized that God had rewarded our diligence and patience with a pair of juvenile black bears. They were playing in the undergrowth, which protected them and obscured our view. After a few minutes, they decided to move and one by one ambled across the road right in front of us.

As we continued our drive, God showed us the Pronghorn Antelope. Later we saw Mule Deer standing knee deep in a creek and a little further on saw a White Tailed Deer grazing in the creek. Surprisingly, instead of eating the grass on the bank, he was putting his nose down into the water, to eat the weed and grasses actually growing under water. In each instance throughout the day, God reserved these wonderful moments just for our pleasure. Many other cars had been in these areas at different times, but each passed us by and left us to witness these magical moments alone.

A few days later, Barb and I decided to head back to the National Bison Range. We had really enjoyed our previous visit and felt blessed by what we had seen, as both of us enjoy wildlife we wanted a second look. As we drove to the park, I quietly asked God if I could see a bison, but this time, up close. They are such magnificent creatures, clearly dangerous but I had a sense they were gentle giants.

On our previous visit we had figured out where the bison were grazing and decided to head out on the shorter drive in the hope of finding them. Once again, we moved very slowly, looking out for anything that moved, we allowed many vehicles to pass us. We rounded a bend and just as I had asked God, off to the right only about fifteen yards off the road we saw one lone bison. We pulled over and stopped to watch and take some photographs. He stood sideways on to us and looked at us over his shoulder, while we took pictures. Then he laid down, there was no grass around him to block our view, and once again he watched us as we photographed him. It was, as if, he were posing for us to allow us time and offer us the best shots. Then as an unforgettable final gift, he rolled on his back and playfully kicked his legs in the air. Several shots later, he had completely disappeared in his own dust cloud. He had finished his show and it was time to leave him alone. As we drove away, we were in awe of this amazing animal and God's incredible gift to us. In all the time we sat and watched him, nobody came by, the whole 'show' was just for us.

We had only just started on the road when this took place and although we could not imagine anything to equal the experience, we decided to continue on our route and complete the journey. This particular road was not a loop. We traveled several miles down the road, then turned around to take the same route back again. We journeyed to the end of the road and were making our way back without seeing anything else.

We were close to where we had previously seen 'our bison model' and saw that a vehicle coming from the opposite direction had stopped. As a bison moved out onto the road, we stopped too. We expected him to cross the road and we would soon continue our journey. However, he walked halfway across and then made a ninety degree turn and set off down the road ahead of us. We moved slowly to follow him at a safe distance, and laughed as we watched a large bison butt sway from side to side in front of us as he made his way down the road. After about twenty yards, he moved slowly off to the side and headed into the undergrowth to graze. We drove by and then pulled up to watch him, wondering if he was the same bison who had posed for us earlier. After the initial vehicle going in the other direction had left, we were once more alone.

We had pulled off the road to the right and Barb, sitting in the passenger seat, reached for her camera to take more pictures through the open car window. After a few minutes, he left his grazing spot and moved back toward the road. He chose a path right alongside the car, so close that Barb could only get his eye and his horn in the picture as he passed. I just stared at the gentle eye of this magnificent animal looking directly at us as he walked by.

We had been amazed by God's gift to us only an hour or so earlier, but God surpassed Himself this time. I had asked God earlier in the day to let me see a bison up close. The lesson I learned from these encounters was 'to be careful what you wish for!' Having said that, they were gifts I would never trade for anything, not only because they were very clearly and specifically, an answer to prayer but also I realized later, that I had no fear. This bison had been close enough for us to touch him and he could easily have destroyed our flimsy car and hurt us had he been inclined to do so. The whole experience was a specific statement to us from God. There was nobody else around on either occasion, in a park, which has hundreds of vehicles driving through it every day. It was as if God had staged the whole event just for our pleasure and both of us felt truly blessed.

We had ventured out on this journey at what we believed to be God's prompting. This experience was a spectacular and unmistakable confirmation that we had been right to make the journey. We were, in fact, where we were supposed to be. Up to this point, we had, had several small events, which showed us that God was guiding and protecting us as we traveled, but this one was truly wonderful. We did not know it at the time, but this was just the first of several encounters with bison. Each were different but equally specific and spectacular. I hope you will enjoy the continuing 'bison saga.'

Many years earlier, we had traveled from Ohio to Oregon, and covered 2,500 miles in only five days. A part of the current journey was to find out what we had missed. After exploring the Mission Valley and visiting Glacier National Park, our next stop was Yellowstone National Park.

While in Yellowstone, we drove through Hayden Valley, where we had been told there was a large herd of bison. The road was relatively quiet but our curiosity was peeked when we spotted a parking lot full of vehicles. As we drove in, we saw a group of photographers with large cameras on tripods, all trained on a herd of bison in the valley below. They all seemed to be waiting for the one moment when something spectacular would happen. Although we did not know it at that moment, we were about to witness God's wonderful sense of humor. Barb pulled into the one remaining parking space and we got out of the car to walk over to the waiting group. I glanced over to my left to make sure Barb was coming to join me. Only a few yards behind her and still approaching, were a pair of bison with a youngster following close behind. I took one quick photo of the approaching family, then retreated behind the car. At the same moment, Barb had spotted the group and ducked back to safety, taking a picture of the family as they passed by. Someone shouted 'move,' and all the photographers in one fluid movement, scooped up their cameras and raced for the safety of the parked cars. The bison family did not break their stride and moments later walked across the ground where the photographers had been congregating, waiting for their 'unforgettable shot of the day.' Ironically, all of them, except Barb and I, missed it.

A little later, we were parked down the road and noticed some unusual movement amongst the herd below us. Some of the bison seemed a little restless and we could see something moving through the group. We got our binoculars and realized that the small grey animal was a coyote working its way through the group. He was alone and I don't think he posed any threat, but he certainly raised their attention level and they moved around restlessly. Although it was a long way off, once again, God had provided us with a unique opportunity and Barb was able to take a picture of the interloper in the herd, before we resumed our journey.

Our final bison encounter would come in Custer State Park. We had seen bison standing, lying down, rolling in the dirt, walking away from us, close up and far away. Unknown to me, as we were driving through Custer State Park, Barb had asked God if she could see one come towards us, to see it 'head on.' A short distance into the park, away from the open range where bison are usually to be found, once again we saw the vehicle coming towards us had stopped. Barb, who was driving, followed suit. We watched as a bison crossed in front of the other vehicle, then made a clear and determined decision to turn toward us. He was on our side of the road and began walking directly towards the car. Watching this animal approach, we could see not just his overall size but the massive, powerful head and shoulders of this creature. Instinctively, I hoped he would not get angry, because if he did, our flimsy vehicle would be history. Barb's camera was inaccessible, but the sunroof was open and she asked me to stand up and take a picture as he approached. I resumed my seat, as he continued to approach us, and was now only a few yards away. Barb considered moving the car over to let him pass, and she asked, "what should we do?" I answered, "keep still!!" Without hesitating, and with remarkable grace for his size, he veered off to the driver's side of the vehicle, missing the wing mirror by no more than a couple of inches, he walked by and continued down the road. Both of us had been holding our breath and breathed a sigh of relief, before driving slowly away. At this point, Barb told me about her earlier prayer to see a bison coming toward us!

When we reached the wildlife section of the park, God rewarded us with many photographic opportunities, beginning with the prairie dogs, which seemed to watch us with the same curiosity as we watched them. We also photographed a whitetail deer grazing at the side of the road and a little further on, a small herd of beautiful pronghorn antelope.

The park was also known for its wild burros and donkeys. We came across a group of mothers and babies taking shade in a small clump of trees. As we got out of the car, I spotted a mother donkey and her foal , both with identical markings. As I looked at them, an image of Jesus filled my mind, as I thought about Him mounting a donkey to enter Jerusalem, and her baby following behind. The markings just seemed to solidify the image in my mind, as I looked at the distinctive black cross on the back and shoulders of both mother and baby. Did Jesus see the same markings on the donkey He rode? I felt God had provided this mother donkey and her foal, just for us, and I was blessed to see them close up, as the mother even allowed me to pet her baby.

We had enjoyed a wonderful time in Custer State Park, but God had one more gift for us. We had previously seen mountain goats, scrambling up the steep cliffs, seemingly finding footholds where they did not exist. Of course, they were in their element, which meant they were always far off and inaccessible. However, as we were heading towards Mount Rushmore, we spotted a mother and baby mountain goat grazing at the side of the road. We got out of the car and walked toward them, being careful not to get too close, as we did not want to stress the mother. She allowed us to take pictures as they continued grazing, undisturbed by our presence. After a few minutes, other people stopped and she had had enough. She walked across the road, with her baby following, and they disappeared into the undergrowth.

As I look back and consider all the close encounters with God's wonderful animals, I am truly amazed. We had visited parks, which attract thousands of tourists, but again and again, we were privileged to see these animals in their own environment, with nobody else around. The bison encounters in particular, seemed to be 'staged' just for our benefit. In every instance, from the bears playfully crossing the road to the deer paddling in the stream; and from the donkeys to the mountain goats, God just put us in the right place at the right time. The wildlife part of our journey was marked with a continuous stream of blessings from God, which left us in no doubt that we were where God wanted us to be.

The next part of our journey led us away from the wilderness as we traveled through Chicago to Ohio. Here we spent time close to family and reconnected with old friends, there was little time to search for wildlife.

As the weather in Ohio turned colder, we set out for a warmer climate and God led us to a quiet, relatively undeveloped part of Florida and the little town of Carrabelle. We had been here several weeks when we received news that a friend from our hometown in Oregon would be passing through and they invited us to their campground for lunch.

My thoughts were so consumed with the carnal pleasure of seeing our friends from Newport, that I almost did not recognize these gifts from God. Several people had told us there were white squirrels in the area but in the time we had been in Carrabelle we had not seen them. We arrived for lunch at the Ochlocknee State Park and as soon as we walked over to our friend's campsite we saw two white squirrels looking down at us from the safety of a tree. Russell coaxed them down with a cracker and they proved to be tame enough to take food from his hand. They entertained us by running up and down the tree trunks, then sitting up, cracker in hand, eating their prize. What a wonderful gift to see these cute little creatures in their own environment.

Later, on our journey home, to complete a perfect day with nature and with friends, we spotted our first Bald Eagle since leaving

Newport. We had visited many places where we were told bald eagles were to be found, but in our whole journey across the country, we had not seen one. Again, we had been told they were in the Carrabelle area, but all we had seen was evidence of empty nests. This day, God rewarded our patience and our diligence with the sight of this majestic bird sitting on the branch of a dead tree, at the side of the road. Although we were on the main road in the area, nobody was around and we were able to stop and take pictures.

I had a sense that God had in some way brought us 'full circle,' by showing us a bald eagle here in our temporary winter home, after driving thousands of miles from our home of fifteen years, which had frequently provided the opportunity to see these magnificent birds. I have no idea what it means, other than it just felt we were in the right place.

Nugget of Information:

Always take the time to see what God has to show you. Everyone else on the road was rushing to the next place, and missed their gift.

CHAPTER SEVEN

Faith Or Religion

Faith versus Religion has been a long standing debate for many years. When I was regularly attending a church, I did not really distinguish between the two. Life in an RV has made it difficult to connect with a church community as we travel from place to place. As I had become separated from the doctrines of religion, I turned to the direct teachings of Jesus, and discovered, what I believe to be the true meaning of Faith. Let me try to explain.

As I was reading John 11 about the death of Lazarus, I came to verses 45-57, which relate to the plot to kill Jesus. The Pharisees had determined that the growing movement by the people to follow Jesus, would threaten their authority and possibly mark the demise of the Jewish Nation at the hands of the Roman Empire.

It did not seem to occur to them, that if Jesus could conquer death itself, by raising Lazarus, then the Romans, who were mere men, would not pose any threat. Instead, they could trust only in their own power, therefore they had to fix the problem themselves. It is not clear to me whether their actions were driven by their own greed and need to maintain their status, purely out of pride, or whether their motive was to protect the Nation of Israel.

Whatever their motive, it is clear they had to be in control, they were unwilling or unable to put their faith in God, the God whom they supposedly served. This led me to consider the fundamental difference between Faith and Religion. It was clearly apparent in Jesus day, and sadly is still apparent today.

Sadly, Christianity today has split into multiple religions, each with their own defined set of beliefs or doctrines. These have been formulated, often over many centuries, by the religious scholars of the day. They are then passed down through the hierarchy of religious leaders and taught to the congregations. These doctrines stand apart from the Word of God and in many respects take priority over the Bible. The services provide members with the 'appropriate' Biblical passages, which have been assigned for the week. There is little or no encouragement to venture beyond these assignments or to indulge in additional, independent study throughout the week.

All of this seems to be very similar to the situation Jesus encountered with the Jewish leaders. Clearly, at that time, the Pharisees were trying to hold together the Jewish Nation, in the face of destruction by the Roman Empire. Except for the major factor that they were completely ignoring the power of God which Jesus had demonstrated, and as such totally lacked faith in God, one could argue the Jewish leaders were justified in their approach. However, religion today does not face any such outside threat. As a result, I can only conclude that their motive is based on a need for power and control.

Faith, on the other hand, is an acknowledgement that God is in control. In truth, everything comes to us from God by Grace, which is a gift freely given. We receive from God through Faith. In other words, Faith appropriates what God has already provided.

It calls us to a personal study of the Word of God and as a result the development of a personal relationship with God. As Rom. 10:17 tells us – "Faith comes by hearing, and hearing by the Word of God." As I mix my faith with the Word of God, then what has already been done by Grace, becomes a reality. In other words, it takes faith to release the Grace of God.

It is this fundamental difference between faith and religion that has drawn me away from organized religion. I have come to a place where religion can provide a valuable sense of community. However, I resist becoming involved with the hierarchy and the politics of the organization. Although I accept the teaching it has to offer, I rely on my own study and prayer life to feed my faith and develop my relationship with God.

Each one of us is in a different place in our journey of life. God has a path for each of us and as such the instruction and guidance we need at any point in time is different. This guidance comes to us directly from the Word of God.

I have come to understand that the Bible is an amazing book to the degree that it can only have come from God. Of course, historically, people set down the words and people determined which books would be included and which would not. However, I have no doubt in my mind that the unseen influence came directly from God through the Spirit at work within the writers and the leaders of the day. There can be no other explanation for the many hidden levels it holds, which are far beyond any human intent or understanding.

On the face of it, to any casual reader, the Bible tells a story, in the Old Testament, of the history of the Jewish Nation. Then the New Testament, contains the story of Jesus and how He came to change the world. It is a powerful book in its own right and provides the basis of Christianity and of belief for those who read it.

However, it holds much more for those who take the time to prayerfully study it and hold themselves open to spiritual direction. Have you ever read a passage in the Bible and then subsequently read it again, only to discover something different from the previous reading? This has always been one of the wonderful miracles of the Bible for me. Sometimes I read and just see the story, later, I read it again and discover a deeper meaning. As I allow myself to be guided by God, a new understanding is revealed to me, even from a passage I thought I knew.

I have come to understand that it is the spirit within me, which teaches me what God wants me to understand, therefore as I am guided to a passage, God reveals its 'hidden meaning' meaning to me. Effectively, I can either choose to read a particular passage and see only the story as written, or I can ask God, what He wants me to learn from the passage and a completely different perspective is revealed.

A wonderful example of this was when I read Mark 11:23-24, in which Jesus said, "If anyone says to this mountain, 'Go, throw yourself into the sea,' and does not doubt in his heart but believes what he says will happen, it will be done for him. Therefore, I tell you, whatever you ask for in prayer, believe that you have received it, and it will be yours."

I have always accepted that God can do anything but this passage has always puzzled me to some degree. I know I have asked God for things, but confess I have always held a grain of doubt to protect myself in case it did not happen, and of course it didn't. However, if I set my own doubt aside, what if I were to ask God for something which would be against God's laws – for example, wish death on someone I did not like? I could not see how that could work.

Taking these verses literally, asking God for something and believing I have received it, would be testing God. What it seems to be saying is, I want something, I just need to have faith and God will give it to me. God has to provide, because this verse says so. NO – the missing piece is that prayer begins with God and God's Grace. By Grace, God provides all I need, then by Faith I appropriate what God has provided. Therefore, I cannot just believe God for a stack of $20 bills and they will appear, because that is not what God's Grace provides for me. If God has not provided for it by Grace, then my Faith cannot make it happen. However, God has promised prosperity and I have faith he will provide for my needs.

The debate over faith versus religion leads to the question – Are these two positions mutually exclusive? The short answer is – they don't have to be. If they were, then I would not be able to attend a church. However, the situation does raise potential problems.

People who attend church will inevitably tell you they are people of faith. Certainly they believe in God and members of the Christian religions believe in Jesus Christ. If that was as far as faith was intended to go, then there would not be an issue. Unfortunately, as I indicated earlier, the different religions operate by their own distinct set of beliefs. In this sense, faith is restricted to the adherence to the doctrines of the particular church. In other words, the rules come first!

One example of potential conflict is in the area of sin, this often means that sin is defined by the church doctrine, in some cases, there are different categories or levels of sin. When someone commits a sin, there is a ritual to seek and receive forgiveness, failure to do so, means condemnation. The individual may even be told they will go to hell if they do not adhere to the perceived 'proper procedures.'

In the Old Testament period, such punishment and cleansing was valid and clearly defined in Mosaic Law. However, we now live in the New Testament era. If we have accepted Jesus Christ as our Savior, then our sins, past, present and future have been forgiven. This is a concept that can be a little difficult to grasp – how can I be forgiven for something I have not yet done? However, if you apply a certain amount of logic to the issue, and consider that Jesus died for our sins over two thousand years ago, then a different perspective must be applied. The action of Jesus' death and resurrection took place long before I was born, therefore, if I am saved by this action, my sins were forgiven before they were committed. Jesus died for the sins of the whole world, before that time; at that time; and for all time, so, a new-criteria for forgiveness must be in place. Without it, then logically Jesus would somehow have to die on the cross after each new sin!

As Jesus died only once, the only way it can possibly work, is that He died for all sin, everywhere and for all time. This is part of the gift from God that we call Grace – it is a gift freely given. Faith is our unconditional acceptance of this gift. By faith we accept and acknowledge the sacrifice of Jesus and as such we are forgiven. If we consider it necessary to go back to God and seek forgiveness each time we sin, then effectively we are saying we do not believe Jesus died for our sins, which negates our faith. A more appropriate response would be to thank God that we are forgiven and ask for guidance to prevent us from repeating our sin.

As I take my faith seriously, I find that I can attend church as an act of praise and worship, and a time to be in God's house. I enjoy the fellowship with people who love God, even if they do not see God in quite the same way I have come to know Him. In this sense, faith and religion can exist side by side.

At the same time, I am aware that generally speaking, religion frowns on the kind of independence I hold, preferring their members to see God in the light of their prescribed doctrines. As such, I have found that faith requires at least a degree of independence from the religious leaders. While it is possible to have both faith and subscribe to a religion, I don't believe it is the norm, because such faith does not meet the prescribed criteria for acceptance by God.

My past experiences with religion have taught me the importance of pursuing my own relationship with God, outside the Church. At the same time, I also know from my own life that the separation also holds potential pitfalls.

Studying the Bible without any guidance to create appropriate 'checks and balances,' I found, made it possible for me to believe I had all the answers. I effectively put myself on equal footing with God. This was based on a skewed logic along the line of - if God lives within me, then I must be equal to God. I found to my chagrin, that taking such a position placed me firmly in the hands of Satan. This twisted logic separated me from God instead of bringing me closer to Him. Satan got into my mind and perpetuated this falsehood. It took me several years, first, to recognize my error and even longer to find my way back. Thankfully, God can turn all situations to good and as a result my faith is now stronger than ever. My understanding is much clearer and having spent time 'in the desert,' I believe I know better than to go back out there again. All the same, I am sharply aware that Satan can and does use any level of weakness to impose his deception and twist the truth. As such, I remain diligent and prayerful, making a conscious effort to not stray from faithful reliance on God.

Faith is about trusting God to take care of you in all situations, particularly when you cannot see the way forward. This journey in our RV has involved many 'faith' moments. I am reminded here, of one amusing experience, and cannot help smiling at both the recollection and at God's sense of humor. We had left the safety of the dealership, where we had stayed for a week and knew that help, when we needed it, was only a phone call and a few minutes away. We traveled back to Newport to complete our business there before beginning our journey. We arrived at the Elks and worked through our checklist to set up the coach for living there for the next couple of weeks.

When we had completed the set up, we realized one of our cats, Patches, was missing. We had previously lost Matt and after a frantic search, had found him under the bed. As a result, we had made a concerted effort to ensure all possible 'cat hiding places' were blocked. However, Patches was missing. We were confident she had not escaped out of the door, as we always carefully closed it behind us, when we went in or out. We knew she must be in the coach somewhere and conducted a careful and thorough search, but without success.

The previous experience with Matt had been traumatic for me, so this time I was leaning heavily on my faith and believing God would work it out. As time went by, we had run out of places to look and it seemed like finding her would be impossible. I left the coach and took a walk in the Elks parking lot. As I walked, I said to God, "Okay God, we could really use a miracle about now!" I returned to the coach. I went in and walked back to the bedroom. At the bedroom door, I turned to say something to Barb and saw Patches casually walking towards me from the front of the coach. She had apparently 'appeared from nowhere.' God's timing is always perfect.

While Patches was missing, I had looked under the dashboard but had seen no sign of her. It was several weeks later, when she went missing again, that we found her hiding place. Under the dashboard at the back was a wooden bulkhead, hiding a small compartment. I shone a flashlight in the small space and saw two bright eyes looking back at me. The mystery was solved, but it was still no less of a miracle, because the timing on the previous occasion was a clear and direct answer to faith and prayer.

Nugget of Information:

Religion and Faith do not have to be mutually exclusive. There are benefits to becoming part of a Church Community. However, I believe it is important to maintain your independence in developing a relationship with God.

CHAPTER EIGHT

How To Pray

I suspect there are almost as many opinions on this subject as there are prayers. I have read books about how to pray, and books which just tell you what to say for each occasion. These are usually very clinical and carefully worded to include the 'appropriate' language.

I have struggled with prayer for years – what should I say? Is it in the correct Biblical language? Did I do it right? Then, of course, there is – did God hear me? Was He pleased or disappointed? Should I say it again, in case He was busy before? Is it okay to ask for things? And if so, How?

I have gone through all of these questions and more. For me, the experience has never been satisfactory. When I have read a prayer, it sounded professional, but it did not come from my heart, therefore at some level it was false. I have tried to make up my own prayers, but was focused on the correct terminology and the word formation, instead of the content. As a result, I never actually relaxed and talked to God.

It has taken me a long time and a lot of searching to understand that it is not about using the right words, it is all about a relationship between God and His people. More significantly, He wants a personal relationship, which means a relationship with me. While I believe it is true that God knows all things and sees all things, and does not actually need a full and accurate commentary on my life, He does want to hear from me. It does not matter how the sentences are formulated. What matters is communication, which comes from my heart.

Sometimes we find ourselves in desperate need or are experiencing physical or emotional pain. On those occasions, in some ways, prayer comes more easily as we are unable to formulate the 'correct' words. In these instances, our prayer always comes from the heart.

The difficulty arises on a day to day basis. Although this is not directly addressing prayer, I think it provides a starting point – Prov. 23:7 – "As he thinks in his heart, so is he."

Each day, I begin my prayer time with thanksgiving. I thank God for the positive experiences of the day and even thank Him for the safe outcome of the negative events of the day. I have found that taking the time each day to express my gratitude to God, leads to my being more thankful in my life. Next, I commit myself, and my day to God, by asking Him to lead me to those people He would have me talk to and give me the words to say. Often this is all I have to say. I no longer spend time trying to think up clever or 'appropriate' words, as I have come to understand that it would only be a selfish ego trip. I don't need to impress God and it does nothing to further my relationship with Him.

Instead, I try, not always successfully, to clear my mind and listen. If I can keep the mundane details of my life from flooding into my mind, then I hear God. It is in these quiet and yet focused times, that God speaks to me. If I am 'wrestling' with something and looking for God to guide me, this is the time I receive clarity. It is not in a voice outside of me, but comes from within. I receive direction and a sense of clarity, it is just an 'inner knowing' about what to do.

I believe prayer should always begin with Thanksgiving and then if I have something on my heart, I can turn my thoughts and prayer to appeal. Jesus gave us specific instruction about this type of prayer. Matt. 7:7-8 – "Ask and it will be given to you; seek and you will find; knock and the door will be opened to you. For everyone who asks receives; he who seeks finds; and to him who knocks, the door will be opened."

These words of Jesus are both specific and clear. Jesus did not say 'ask, and if it does not happen immediately, ask again and again,' He did not tell us to ask and if our prayer is not answered, tell all your friends and get them to keep bombarding heaven with the same request until God listens and moves. Sadly, perhaps due to lack of understanding, we have added to Jesus words.

Part of the problem with our assumption that we must keep repeating our appeal to God is that most of us remain one hundred percent in our carnal world. On my part, as I have stated, I did not understand the concept of the spiritual realm. I certainly did not understand how I can and do function in both the physical and spiritual world.

When our mind only recognizes the physical world, we are forever 'trying to get God to come here and do things for us.' If you think about this in terms of relationship, it is very one-sided and selfish. If you think about making a new friend and the friend always wants you to go to his or her house and do what he or she wants, how would you feel and react? At some point, you would want your new friend to visit and hang out with you. Friendship or relationship is 'a two-way street.'

The revelation for me, came as I began to understand and believe in the spirit realm. This is when I realized I can just 'hang out' with God. The greatest gift God had for me, was the gift of the Holy Spirit. As the Holy Spirit is from God, it is the key to the spirit world. It is the Holy Spirit who opens the hidden secrets of the Word of God and teaches us about the spiritual part of our self.

Jesus taught in parables, instead of straight talk, and He told the disciples in Mk. 4:11-12 – "The secret of the Kingdom of God has been given to you. But to those on the outside everything is said in parables, so that, 'they may be ever seeing but never perceiving, and ever hearing but never understanding; otherwise they might turn and be forgiven.'"

Before His crucifixion, Jesus promised to send a Counselor to help us and show us the way. John 14:26 – "The Counselor, the Holy Spirit, whom the Father will send in my name, will teach you all things and will remind you of everything I have said to you." Although we recognize this in theory, we rarely embrace Him to learn all He can teach and show us.

In my prayer and study, these things started to come together like the pieces of a puzzle. God led me to study some of Andrew Wommack's books (A Better Way to Pray) and the missing pieces fell into place.

I have no idea how it works, but in my tiny mind, I look at the spirit world as a parallel universe with our physical world. God lives in the spirit world, although on occasions performs miracles in our world.

God can, of course, do anything, but He will only act in accordance with His own established Laws of God. God will not give you something, which is contrary to His own laws. For example, asking God to kill someone's wife, so that you can have her husband, is not going to work.

Consider that, God answers our prayer immediately, therefore, when we ask God for something, it is instantly provided in the spirit world, where God is. However, there is a second part, which is variable, and this is the manifestation of our answered prayer into the physical world. This is the part we do not recognize.

Once you accept the concept that your prayer is immediately answered in the spirit world, then to ask again demonstrates lack of faith. Jesus died for our sins only once and made us a promise that our prayers would be answered. So to ask over and over is to effectively try to have Jesus crucified over and over, to make our appeal work. When I first heard this idea, I was horrified with myself, for my actions!

The first step then, is to Ask. Next is to have faith and believe. Sometimes our prayer is answered quickly, but other times it appears that our appeal has been lost. Jesus prompted us to Seek. The only place I know of to 'seek' is in the Word of God, ensure that your request is in accordance with God's Law. God will not break His own Laws to accommodate your selfish desire. Then stay focused on God's Word. It is not so much about looking for a specific answer, although such an answer may manifest, it is about keeping Satan at bay.

Satan, unfortunately is alive and well. His strength comes from deceit and lies. When we pray for something in earnest and are waiting for its manifestation, Satan goes to work. He tries to break your faith by filling your mind with doubt and encouraging you to ask again for something God has already given. He may even delay the manifestation by interfering with people on whom the answered prayer depends. For example, if you are selling your house and ask God for help, Satan may sidetrack the buyer, God has chosen. This is a delaying tactic and cannot ultimately stop God, but it may disrupt things enough, for you to doubt God.

Throughout this waiting time, seeking and staying in God's Word is vital. It cements our faith in the outcome. It may also provide us with prayerful direction. Instead of going back to God and 'asking' again, acknowledge that your prayer has been answered in the spirit world. Ask God to manifest your answered prayer into our physical world or to show you the cause of the delay and what, if anything, you can do to make a difference. God may show you that Satan is interfering.

Remember, that Jesus showed us through the disciples that God has given us the power to defeat Satan. It states in Matt .10:1 – "He called his twelve disciples to him and gave them authority to drive out evil spirits and to heal every disease and sickness." Then later Paul in Eph. 6:10-17 directed us to put on the full armor of God so that we can stand against the devil's schemes. It is no longer up to God to stop Satan, through the name of Jesus that power has been given to each one of us. Instead of praying and asking God to take away the problem, we can and should cast out the devil ourselves, using the name of Jesus. Whenever, I consider that my prayer has not manifested into this world due to Satan's interference, I pray a simple prayer. Something like, 'I believe God has already provided *xyz* but it has not yet manifested into my world, I command you Satan to get out of the way of its manifestation, in the name of Jesus Christ. Amen.'

After we have Asked, we should follow Jesus instructions and Seek. Then God, through the Holy Spirit will lead us to Find the way for our prayer to manifest into our physical world. Instead of asking over and over, I encourage you to believe your prayer has been answered and ask only for help in its manifestation.

I have to say that these revelations regarding how to pray were new to me also. The idea and the process do not yet come naturally to me and I have to catch myself when I drift back to 'the old way' of prayer. Thankfully, we have an understanding God and I get back on track.

As Barb and I have journeyed across the U.S., God has been teaching me what I need to know and how to rely on Him. As we have been apart from family and friends, our usual support group has been almost non-existent. As a result, it has been a natural step to turn to God.

As I have previously stated I try to take time each day to read and study the Word and to pray. Our path has been fairly clear, with few life decisions, so my prayers have been those of thanksgiving and turning over the day to God and asking Him to Guide me in His ways.

However, I remember one particular occasion, when we were in leaving Joliet, Illinois. We had an appointment to have work done on the coach, in Nappanee, Indiana and it was time to leave. The timing was tight for our journey as we were scheduled for an early morning appointment.

The night before our departure, Barb had suffered a bout of food poisoning and as we settled down to sleep, she was as white as a sheet. At any other time, I would have been both concerned for her well-being and stressed out by trying to figure out a 'plan B,' having already decided the likelihood of traveling the next day was slim.

Instead, I turned all my energy to prayer. In Matt. 10:1 Jesus told us we have been given the power to heal. As I had learned it, a gift given to us by the Holy Spirit must be embraced and used, instead of begging God for something we have already received. I prayed, commanding the healing Barb had already received to manifest into our world, in Christ's name. Then, I went to sleep believing 'it was a done deal.' Barb slept well and in the morning all trace of her sickness had passed.

We programmed Grace (our GPS) and set off on our journey. Fortunately, Barb was well rested and fully recovered as the journey had its challenges. Barb did a great job following Grace's instructions, but knew little about the programming side. Unfortunately, the rough road bounced us around and the program was lost. If Barb had still been sick, this could have been very difficult, but she simply followed my verbal directions and quickly got Grace back on track.

We had not been to the Newmar factory before, but had been told there were a number of full hookups at the Service Department and an overflow with limited service nearby. God continued to take care of us on our arrival. When we pulled into the parking lot, someone came over to help us and noticed there was one pull through slot left. As my skills in backing into a slot were still limited, this was a relief, and we quickly settled in. Not only had God ensured a space for us, He had found an easy spot for us, after a long drive.

You could argue that I don't really know whether Barb would have been okay the next day anyway. However, I know her body does not normally recover from a bout of sickness quickly, she usually takes several days to recover. This experience was a very clear demonstration of God's healing power, in my eyes. It has given me a different perspective on how to pray and as long as it is accompanied by belief, it is clearly highly effective.

In summary, command in Christ's name and pray from belief it is already done, not from request. Understand that God is in the spirit realm and all prayer has been answered immediately in His realm. It is our belief which brings the answered prayer and manifests it into our physical world. Most important to understand is that asking over and over for the same thing, is actually a demonstration of lack of faith.

Nugget of Information:

As long as your prayer is in accordance with God's Laws, once you have Asked, your prayer has been answered in the spirit world. All future prayer must be directed towards the manifestation of your prayer into our physical world. This may involve commanding the devil to 'get out of the way,' or seeking guidance from God to reveal the cause of the delay.

CHAPTER NINE

Wisdom Of The Spirit

One of the unexpected aspects of the RV life for me, has been the freedom of my mind. As I am no longer distracted by the daily challenges of home ownership and routine, I seem able to focus more clearly on God in my life.

I have previously stated that as a born again Christian, I am one third Holy Spirit. From the beginning, I accepted this in principle and understood it as a foundational change within me. Intellectually, I was no longer destined to live a carnal life. I realized that through the study of God's Word, I could retrain my mind to focus on God and overcome my carnal nature.

Slowly, I have become more comfortable with the concept of the spiritual part of me and connecting with the spirit realm. As such, I am beginning to connect more with God and as a result develop a closer relationship with God.

It is now becoming clear to me that the power of the Holy Spirit within me has much more to offer. As I read the Bible, I seem to see more and understand better. It is like the difference between looking across a field on a foggy day and looking at the same scene on a bright clear day.

John 14:26 tells us, "The Holy Spirit whom the Father will send in my name, will teach you all things, and remind you of everything I have said to you." It is the job of the Holy Spirit to give me revelation knowledge. It reveals the truths written in the Bible. I have come to understand that the Bible was written to my heart, not to my brain, therefore no amount of intellectual analysis will provide its true meaning. It is the Holy Spirit which provides the translation and as a result, the revelation knowledge.

As I now study the Bible with the benefit of insight through the Holy Spirit within me, I find myself reading verses, which have long been familiar to me, but with a new perspective. In the past, they have been merely words on the page, a part of a story, and sometimes it seemed an odd diversion from the point. Now, I have new clarity.

Recently, I read 1 Cor. 2:9 – "No eye has seen, no ear has heard, no mind has conceived what God has prepared for those who love him." This used to be a verse, which seemed to be a promise of things to come. I considered that someday in the future, when I got to heaven, I would finally understand the mysteries of God. On this occasion, I viewed it from a whole new perspective. The Spirit within, showed me that this promise is available to us here and now.

God had used His spiritual 'key' to unlock the meaning of His Word. Its purpose is to guide me into a deeper relationship with Him, because without understanding there can be no relationship.

This revelation means that I can choose to focus on living through my spiritual self, which will connect me more closely with God, instead of focusing on living only through my carnal self. As a result, my attention and energy has shifted from acting and reacting to the physical senses and allowing my mind to be pulled by my emotions. Instead, I am now retraining my mind, through reading God's Word, to rely on the promises of God and be directed through faith in Him. I am learning to reject negative emotions, as I understand them to be driven by outside influences designed to separate me from trust and reliance on God.

Making the choice to live a spiritual life has for me, become 'a work in progress.' Although I think I understand in principle, it can be a challenge to maintain this direction in practice. In fact, I believe this is part of the reason for writing this book. It is as much to do with my own understanding as sharing my story with you.

Clearly, even after making the choice to become more spiritual, this has to be done in the physical world and as such, I must find a balance between the two. In truth this is a daily challenge I have lived so many years with only an understanding of my physical world, I quickly default back to what I know when faced with a problem or a question.

However, as I study more and spend more time in God's Word, my mind is becoming more attuned to God's prompting. I already have an inner sense of God's prompting on occasion. In fact, this book and its content, have come solely out of God's prompting. I have sudden and unexpected revelations for chapter titles, and then again as I sit and stare at the blank page. When I start typing the words are formed without thought or planning.

While the writing is clearly spirit driven and automatic, I still need to hone the skill when it comes to everyday life. Each morning, I place my life and my day in God's hands, asking Him to guide me wherever He wants to lead me. Occasionally, at the end of the day, I have a sense that I have done God's work, often I do not. However, I also understand that nobody knows what or who they have influenced, so I may not know the difference one kind word has made in someone's life.

Of course, life in the physical world, requires that we make choices and decisions each day. Daily living seems to be full of options, these may be simple, like eating chicken or fish for lunch, or highly complex. When it comes to the important choices, I used to find myself stressing out over, 'what does God want me to do?' I would pray for guidance, then second guess myself, wondering if it was really God or was it really just my decision.

Thankfully, God has been leading me to a solution to this ongoing problem. Now, when I am faced with one of life's choices, I prayerfully consider the pros and cons of each option, and then choose the one, which gives me the greatest sense of peace.

Remember, as long as you are doing what God has told you to do, He will protect you. However, we must always exercise caution, and take care not to take matters into our own hands. God calls us to rely on Him, not take His idea and then go out and make it happen our way, under our own power.

The easiest way to remember this fact is to always remember, 'God is not going to fund your Ishmael. If you go out and have an Ishmael, you will have to feed him.' This concept is based on the story of Abraham, in which God promises him that he will have a son. As he believes Sarah is too old to bear a child, he goes out and has a son, Ishmael, with his servant. God refuses to allow His covenant to pass through Ishmael as Abraham had hoped. Subsequently God gives Abraham and Sarah their promised child, Isaac, and it is Isaac who bears God's covenant.

Clearly, we are called to listen for God's prompting and to follow it, however unlikely it may appear to be. I am still learning to recognize God's prompting, but I have found that, even if the right direction is not clear, there is a dis-ease associated with the wrong direction, if I keep myself open. In other words, 'follow your heart,' if you have peace in your heart, it is God's guidance.

Towards the end our stay in Waynesville, Ohio, we were considering where we should travel for the winter. Obviously, we needed to head south, but where. We were not sure whether we wanted to travel around, or find a place to stay for several months.

Fellow campers in various places had previously given us their advice and suggestions. We had people tell us to head into central or southern Florida to be sure of escaping the cold weather. Barb wanted to see the Gulf and people recommended the Mobile, Alabama area or the western part of the panhandle of Florida. Friends we had met on our travels recommended Arizona or southern Texas. We were not short of recommendations or advice.

It was time to work through the suggestions and figure out the right place for us. Initially, we considered the options from a practical perspective. We decided Texas and Arizona involved too much traveling, we were ready to rest awhile. When we checked into central and southern Florida, we found that the temperature stayed in the eighties by day and around seventy at night. We also found out it was a very desirable area and as such very expensive. We actually preferred cooler weather anyway and decided somewhere on the Gulf coast would work for us.

I honestly cannot say that I started out by asking God for guidance, but in hindsight, He was clearly part of the process. We continued our search, by checking out numerous RV parks in the Mobile Bay area and then into the Western Panhandle. We rejected each one, often without any rational explanation, it 'just did not feel right.' Our research took us further east and we came across the town of Carrabelle, Florida. Nobody in our travels had even mentioned this area, so we had no information about it. Here, we found three resorts and checked each online. Until this time, we had not stayed at a park with concrete pads and we had this as one of our aims. Only one of the three locations had concrete pads, it was close to the Gulf, but not too close, and there was a National Forest around it. This spot just felt right and when we called, they had space for us for three months.

When we finally arrived there about a month later. It was quiet and isolated, Barb was concerned it would be too quiet, but God soon took care of that. We decided to go to church one Sunday, and although it was small, it became a 'gateway' into the community. As we met more people, we settled in and it soon became 'a home away from home.'

Now, the experience I have related here was not dominated by a sense of God's guidance throughout the process, although the final choice gave us a sense of peace. Interestingly, after we had been in Carrabelle for a while and had settled, we began to realize just how much God had taken care of us. First, we heard from our Arizona friends, who lamented about how cold it had been. Then a friend in Southern Texas told us about the floods in her area. Later, we met someone who had come through the Mobile Bay area and told us about four tornados in their area. As we watched the weather news, we could see major storms traveling from west to east along the Gulf Coast, with lots of rain and lightening. These storms affected just about every area to our west, but by the time they reached Carrabelle they had diminished to just an inch or two of rain.

As we looked at all the severe weather to the west of us, we prayed for the safety of the people located in those areas and thanked God that He had kept us out of the area. At the same time, He had brought us into a place, where the people accepted us and made us part of their community. God has brought us to a place of safety and peace.

As an added bonus, God connected us with a community within our RV Park. We discovered a group of people who returned for several months each year, and they welcomed us into their community with open arms.

This has been a time for me to listen to God's prompting and follow His direction. During the last two months, I have spent time reading and studying God's Word. I am slowly becoming more attuned to the Wisdom of God's Spirit within me and I am daily aware of His has guidance as I write.

Nugget of Information:

Choosing to live through one's spiritual self, instead of only our carnal self, is making a commitment to listen for and follow God's prompting. It is not deciding on the right thing to do and then expecting God to make it work for you.

CHAPTER TEN

Fruit of The Spirit

Life in an RV is very different from what may be called 'conventional living.' We have discovered that our priorities have changed, and our sense of what is important takes on new meaning.

When we lived in Newport in a regular house, we had no concerns about where we were, daily life had its own routine, as long as we paid our bills, heating was just a matter of turning a dial and water, just turning on a faucet.

As we traveled across the country in the RV, even though our bed moved with us, we still had to find a safe place to park each night. A routine that works in one place, may need to change at the next stop. Although we travel with our own supply of water and the ability to cook; heat the coach; and operate the lights, this is more of an emergency fallback than a way of life. So far, we have successfully found an RV Park wherever we have stopped. This brings its own challenges, navigating into the parking slot; connecting to the electric and water supplies; and handling our own sewage disposal in a timely manner.

After a long journey across country, we have chosen to stay at the same location in Florida for the winter months and we thought this would afford us the opportunity to settle into a fixed routine again, at least for a while. However, a cold weather snap changed things again. What are considered simple systems in a home, can become a challenge with an RV. For example, as the temperature dropped, we realized that it would be wise to disconnect our water supply. A hose-pipe connection, is not advisable in freezing weather.

I have always been a person who lived an organized and predictable life. I liked to plan for all eventualities, considering as many variations as possible, to protect against every unforeseen circumstance. I used to pride myself on being a master at 'what-ifs.'

God has turned all these self-imposed standards upside down by placing me in an RV. This lifestyle is, by necessity, one continuous variable. It is impossible to rely on any plan, however carefully formulated, as everything is subject to change. This is the most unlikely way of life, that anyone who knows me, would expect me to adopt. And yet, here I am and I am loving it.

The only way this could possibly work was for me to let go of my need to be in control, give myself over to God, and have faith in His plan for me. Now each morning, I place myself in His hands, ask Him to guide me in all I do and say. In fact, this has become the sum total of my daily plan and as I complete my prayer time, I am blessed with an undeniable sense of Peace.

Peace, of course, is one of the Fruits of the Spirit. The Bible identifies the fruit of the Sprit in Gal. 5:22 – "The fruit of the Spirit is love, joy, peace, patience, kindness, goodness, faithfulness, gentleness, and self-control."

Peace is a recurring theme in the Bible, but can appear contradictory depending upon the passage. At the time of Jesus' birth, in Luke 2:14 the angels declared, "Glory to God in the highest and on earth peace, good will to men." This was a declaration from God that peace had been restored between God and man. No longer would man's sin be counted against them. On the other hand, in Matthew 10:34-36 Jesus talks about the fact that He 'did not come to bring peace but a sword.'

Careful reading of Jesus' words shows us that following Jesus may not 'sit well' with one's fellow men. In other words, not all men are ready to follow Jesus and may create conflict with those who do.

I have come to understand that the peace I experience, is between myself and God. I take every opportunity to gently share that peace, often with a simple heartfelt, 'Bless You.' Beyond that, it is up to God because only God can reach into the heart of a person and wake up their longing for God. If I strive to live out my life trying to reflect God's peace and love, maybe it will strike a chord in those who cross my path.

There is a simplicity about our new lifestyle which is freeing. We meet people from all different walks of life, often with unknown varying political and economic agendas. Different people cross our paths each day and remain in our realm of contact for days or weeks. Some have become friends and we have remained in contact after parting ways, others are simply like 'ships passing in the night.' I have no idea what impression I have made on those I have met and do not have to worry about it, as the connection is only temporary. This means, I have no need to be anything other than my authentic self. There is no pressure to impress and therefore no stress.

This ability to be who I am without concern has become an environment in which the Fruits of the Spirit can thrive unabated. As our lifestyle is one of limited structure, each new encounter is an opportunity to share our experiences. As our journey has been centered around God, I usually find an opportunity to share the miracles, from my heart. For me at least, this is the essence of the fruit of the Spirit within me.

I rarely try to analyze the individual characteristics of the fruit of the spirit, but this would seem to be a good place to consider them one at a time.

Love, is usually mentioned as part of the Christian life. Jesus calls us to 'love one another,' and it is a theme, which runs through His ministry. As much as we hear about 'love,' it often seems to be in short supply in the lives of many Christians. We are caught up in a busy world, in which little time is given in consideration of others. Most people today are too focused on self and their own agendas as they seek happiness. However, love by its very nature requires the focus to be on 'the other person.' The definition of Love is a sacrificial act; an unmerited deed to help a person in need. The irony of this situation is that few realize in giving love, one invariably receives love and experiences the pleasure they have been seeking within themselves. In other words, love brings its own reward!

This leads us conveniently to Joy. Joy has been defined as an inner happiness not dependent on outward circumstances. This is most clearly seen in Paul's letter to the Philippians. Paul is clearly in prison, but in Phil. 1:4 he says, 'I always pray with Joy......'

As I sit here trying to find words to explain an experience of Joy, God brought to my mind a time in my life over twenty years ago. It was the first Christmas after the death of my husband. Shortly after he died, I experienced a very intense presence of God, which, with the guidance of my priest, led me into a relationship with God. Ted had died in March, and I was conflicted as Christmas approached. On the one hand, it would be the first Christmas without Ted in twenty-five years, and at the same time, it was the celebration of my Lord's birth. I had no idea how I would feel on Christmas morning. When I woke up, I was overwhelmed by a sense of joy that filled my whole being. I remember making a conscious effort to stop myself from literally climbing on the roof to shout for joy to the whole neighborhood. The feeling completely consumed me, and 'spilled out' to those around me, much to their confusion. My friends had expected me to be sad and depressed, but my joy could not be denied.

In my experience, Joy is not a conscious emotion. It is not generated within one's carnal self. Joy comes directly from the Spirit, and in my experience at least, overtakes the body and mind without consideration for the physical circumstances.

Patience, is one of the fruits of the Spirit, that has grown within me as I have walked with God. Patience is putting up with others, even when one is severely tried. My greatest challenge in remaining patient, has been when trying to resolve a problem with a customer service person on the phone. I find it difficult being tolerant with incompetence and the bureaucracy of 'jumping through hoops' for the sake of it. This is an area, God still has work to do with me, but I have noticed, that my tolerance level continues to grow in this area.

Kindness, in some respects seems to be related to patience. It is defined as doing thoughtful deeds for others, but I have noticed within myself that I tend to be more calm and thankful in my interactions with people. In today's society, everyone seems focused on complaining about everything, and I find a kind word is a blessing in its own right. I now make a conscious effort to show kindness and gratitude towards those I meet.

Goodness is showing generosity to others. Once again, I believe this should be an integral part of one's connection with people in daily life.

The fruit of the Spirit is referring to how the Spirit changes us and how we interact with our fellow man, not how we act towards God. Therefore, faithfulness in this sense is not about our faith in God, it is about our trustworthiness and reliability in our own behavior. I have always considered my trustworthiness and reliability as important factors to my personal integrity. As I have always held my integrity in the highest esteem, this has not really been an issue in my life. However, as I now reflect upon it as one of the fruits of the Spirit, this has given me a different perspective. I had always considered faithfulness as something exclusively related to God, therefore, I have never considered these qualities as faithfulness.

The last two fruits of the Spirit are Gentleness and Self-Control. They are defined as meekness and humility, and victory over sinful desires. I have linked these two because my issues with self-control in the past tended to be in the realm of anger control. I would remain calm for a period and then explode. I have never been violent, but my mother would tell people, I could give 'a tongue-lashing' second to none. This is an English phrase to describe a verbal tirade, designed to reduce the recipient to total defeat. In other words, in the past, my gentleness and self-control had its limitations! Nowadays, I am still not perfect, but I am much slower to anger.

When I started this review of the Fruits of the Spirit, I had no idea where it may lead. It began more as an academic exercise than self-analysis, but clearly God had other ideas. In considering this passage, word-by-word and how it relates to me on a personal level, I have discovered more clearly, how God has and continues to work in and through me. Looking back, I never made a conscious decision to change and become more patient, or kind, or anything else. It has become clear that the Fruit of the Spirit is beyond my control, it has come directly from God. Through the Spirit, which lives within me, God has instilled in me new qualities. They did not occur due to a change in my carnal self, making a decision to try harder to be a good person. They are the result of the spirit instilling these qualities into my mind, which have resulted in a change in both my carnal mind and body.

I started this chapter based on a word from God that it was the next chapter heading. I had no conscious direction and no miracle from our journey to explain it. Now, I see that the writing of it, is the miracle. It demonstrates how, if we allow it, we can take a word from God and go where it leads us. It shows how focusing on a passage, word by word, instead of just as a whole, can hold its own personal message.

In my recent study about meditation, as I discussed earlier, this is the method I used. I believe this happened to me in writing about the Fruit of the Spirit. God provided a practical example by directing me into a meditation and showing me how the Spirit can influence my carnal mind and move my body in a new direction.

Nugget of Information:

Just as fruit is the end result in the growing cycle of a plant, so too, is the Fruit of the Spirit the end result of the spirit's growth within. In other words, Peace, Love, Joy, Patience, Kindness, Goodness, Gentleness and Self-Control, come from the Spirit living within you. They are not attributes from your carnal self.

CHAPTER ELEVEN

God & Encounters With Nature

This journey in our RV has, for me, been about finding God and it would not be complete without recognizing the natural wonders, which have surrounded us on our travels. One of the easiest places to find God is in nature. All we need to do is to open our eyes and just look around. As carnal human beings we often look at what we have created or achieved and proudly acknowledge these 'things' for their beauty. In truth, they can never 'hold a candle,' to the things of God's creation.

When we lived in Oregon, we witnessed the awesome power and beauty of God's creation on a regular basis. We saw the sunrise over the hills to the east of our home and watched magnificent sunsets over the Pacific Ocean to our west. A continuing source of wonder to us was the changing moods of the ocean. On some days it would be glassy calm and sapphire blue, while on others it would be steel grey in color, and on stormy days the calmness was replaced with raging waves and churning surf.

We knew our journey across the country would be one of new sights and new experiences, but I was not really prepared for the wonders of nature that God had in store for us.

As we traveled, we saw how the Columbia River had carved a deep passage through the rocks to create the Gorge. We saw the fertile valleys in eastern Washington and beautiful rivers and waterfalls in Idaho. Although we acknowledged these on our travels, God had so much more to show us.

We journeyed to Polson, Montana in the Mission Valley, at the southern edge of Flathead Lake. This area was beautiful in its own right, but the main reason for our stop was to visit Glacier National Park. We arrived there during a period of drought and forest fires. All week we had been observing the smoky haze in the mountains and hoped for a clear day. Finally, we just decided to drive up to Glacier and trust God would show us what He wanted us to see. Up in the mountains, it was clear and sunny. Later we heard that the smoke had settled in the valley that day, and learned it had not been coming from the fire on the east side of Glacier National Park as we had assumed, but from fires to the west in Washington State.

As we drove up in the mountains, we began to get a sense of the vastness and wonder of God's creation. We looked around us, and saw magnificent, naturally carved rocks, looking like giant cathedrals. I was reminded of the cathedral buildings in Britain, as I looked at the sheer rock faces, with their deeply carved crevices. However, these natural creations were vast and magnificent in their size and beauty.

106

Thousands of feet up and off in the distance were glaciers nestled in the rocks. I found myself staring at them and trying to wrap my brain around the fact that, ice fields existed so high up, much closer to the sun than we were, and we were enjoying 80 degree temperatures. I could only begin to imagine how thick the ice must be to have remained there without melting, perhaps since the last ice age.

These and many other visions overloaded my small brain as we drove for miles and found new spectacular views around each bend. Glacier National Park left me in awe of God's creation as I began to realize and accept that on the road we traveled, I was seeing only a miniscule portion of the whole.

When we left Polson, we made our way to Yellowstone National Park and the home of 'Old Faithful.' Of course, we had seen pictures of the famous geyser, but seeing it for ourselves was totally different. The Old Faithful geyser has been exploding with boiling water and steam, about 180 feet into the air like clockwork for years. It is so predictable that the park rangers, post a schedule at the park entrance. There were numerous geysers all around the park, some just spewing water and steam, others smelled like rotten eggs and left a telltale yellow sulfur stain on the surrounding rocks. However, the other geysers did not have a particular schedule, only Old Faithful seemingly worked to a timetable. I have seen many examples of God's creativity and His power, particularly after living on the Oregon coast, but this was an awesome sight. It became even more amazing as we walked around the visitors' center and gained insight into what was actually happening beneath our feet.

We discovered that we were actually standing in the caldera of a huge volcano. In fact, virtually the whole park was a caldera. We had been witnessing the effects of the natural heat from the underlying rocks. It boiled the water in an underground pool until the pressure built to the point of forcing steam and boiling water out of the ground in a huge fountain. The scientists were still not certain why Old Faithful was predictable, when the other geysers were not. However, they speculated that once it 'blew,' the water fell and made its way back down into its own pool to begin the process again. The other geysers in the park were believed to draw their water from a common water source, which made them unpredictable.

Once we got over the slightly unnerving feeling of standing in the caldera of an active volcano, the details surrounding the geology of Yellowstone Park were fascinating. Somehow, knowing what was happening and how the huge fountain of water was formed, increased the wonder of God's mighty power.

We left the wonders of Yellowstone and headed to Mount Rushmore and Custer State Park. God had already shown us the distinctive shapes of the tall, sharp edged mountains of Glacier National Park. Next, in Custer State Park, we saw the huge rounded boulders and spires of grey rock, with massive cracks and fissures, which made up the distinctive mountains of this region. Once again we were in awe of God's creation and the sheer scale of these rock formations. The spires were so vast that a tunnel, big enough to drive a large truck through it, had been cut in the base of one of the rocks, and yet it looked small in relationship to the huge rock formation.

As we continued our exploration of this area, we visited both Mount Rushmore and the Crazy Horse monument. Each of these provided a man-made vision on an enormous scale. However, neither would have been possible without the vast mountains, which provided the 'blank canvas' for these incredible projects.

We had visited several parks in different areas but one thing stood out which tied all of them together. The forces of nature which God had used in forming His wonderful creation, as well as the scale on which it had all come into being was truly awesome. The majestic, cathedral like mountains of Glacier National Park stand as a witness to God's amazing creation. Equally, the amazing sight of the Old Faithful geyser is a living demonstration of God's infinite power. The mountains in the Custer State Park area were on a scale difficult to wrap the mind around, especially when you understand that the faces of the presidents on Mount Rushmore were over sixty feet tall and the face of Crazy Horse was even bigger, as it topped one hundred feet. In each instance, looking at these monuments takes your breath away, not just for man's contribution, but for God's initial contribution in providing the 'canvas,' which made them possible.

As our travels continued our encounters with nature were not limited to the mountains, glaciers and the geysers. A huge part of God's creation is found in the daily occurrences, particularly the weather and we were thankful that God was at the center of our journey, to protect us through all of our weather challenges.

I have already mentioned our encounters with crosswinds in the Columbia River Gorge and bouts of heavy rain on the highways. Let me share with you some of the other ways in which God protected us in our encounters with nature as we traveled.

We had made our way across the country and were finally heading towards Ohio, where the kids lived. We had planned to stay at the

FMCA Park near Cincinnati for a few days, while we checked out long-term parks closer to Lebanon. At the last minute, we were able to get into a park in Waynesville, which put us close to the family and saved us driving into the Greater Cincinnati area. We were already grateful to God for finding us a good spot. However, our gratitude increased when we saw the local news that evening. We knew there were storms and heavy rain in the area, but we were shocked when the newsman announced a flood warning for the area where we would have traveled to the FMCA Park. We did not know if the park itself was flooded, but given Barb's knowledge of Cincinnati, the area around it would definitely have been flooded. Once again, God had protected us from a stressful situation at best, and possibly much worse.

While we were staying in Waynesville, we experienced a couple of cold nights, freezing and a little below. Remember, life in a motorhome was still a new experience for us, and although we knew we would have heat to keep us warm, there were other considerations.

A few weeks earlier, when we had stopped at Newmar, the manufacturer of our coach, to have some minor problems addressed. I had the presence of mind to ask a few questions about cold weather at the time. We had been advised to use the heat pads on the tanks and switch on the furnace to prevent the pipes from freezing.

When we heard the forecast, we followed the advice from the Newmar technician. As we prepared, God told me to go outside and disconnect the water pipe at both ends, as this would protect both the coach and the main stand-pipe. We thought we had covered everything, but the next morning, we had a stream of water running across the floor, apparently from the Refrigerator. It was a Saturday morning and Newmar was closed, so I called, Roger. He was our salesman from back in Oregon, who had helped us numerous times by answering questions as we traveled. On this occasion, he reminded me about the outside refrigerator panel and with his guidance, I found the leaking connection. He gave me instructions on how to safely tighten the loose connection without doing any damage. He also advised me to switch the refrigerator from electric to propane on cold nights, as the heat generated would keep the area behind the panel warm and prevent the problem in the future. The next night it was 28 degrees, but God had educated us and led us to the right people to prevent any further problems.

We left Waynesville towards the end of October and headed back to Newmar for some maintenance work before traveling down to Florida for the winter. Although we did not realize it at first, God effectively rearranged our whole travel schedule. The work to be done at Newmar took a day longer than planned and delayed our departure day to Thursday. This turned out to be a blessing as there was a warning that the remnants of a recent hurricane would be moving into the area. The forecast was for strong winds, which would have made traveling difficult, to say the least, if we had been on the road. We decided to stay another day in the safety of Newmar's camping facility and we finally left on Friday, after the weather system had passed through.

We finally arrived in Florida and after months of travel and thousands of miles, we are grateful that God has cared for us along the way. He has shown us some amazing sights, kept us safe as we traveled through adverse weather conditions and protected us from situations that we could not have prepared for in advance. We are here in Carrabelle, Florida for the winter months with time to rest and

111

relax after our long journey. However, we know that God does not rest and is still accompanying us through our days of fun and exploration.

God was even with me this morning as I walked on the beach. I watched one of the small shore birds, running along at the water's edge. He ran a few feet, then stopped to dig in the sand with his beak. The waves here are only a few inches high, but would easily knock this small bird off his feet. I watched and waited for the seemingly inevitable moment when he would be 'bowled over' by an incoming wave. As I observed his movements, he would dig until the last possible moment, then run to safety. I have no idea how he knew, not only the exact location of each wave, but also, how far it would come ashore. As I watched this carefully choreographed dance, I could only conclude that God had instilled into this tiny little bird, some kind of sixth sense to keep him safe. This was irrefutable evidence that God loves even the tiniest creatures in His creation.

In truth God is wherever we look for Him. One of the blessings of our journey is that I seem to be more attuned to God and as a result I am able to see him in even the smallest actions and circumstances. In some respects, we seem to expect God to be a part of nature and perhaps that makes Him easier to find and to accept. I have related here some of my experiences of God's presence in the natural but I have found Him on the road and in securing a safe place to stay for us for the night. I believe, the key is to expect to see God working in all that you do and actively look for the ways He is influencing your life. Miracles are to be found in the everyday activities of life, not just in big 'earth moving' events. I have found that in order to see God's miracles, your heart and mind must be open to receiving them.

Nugget of Information:

We have been blessed to see many wonderful sights on our travels, but there is one common thread, which runs through everything. This has to be the awesome size and grandeur of God's Creation. We, as human beings like to tell ourselves that we are the masters, but after seeing what God has done, I am left in no doubt that we could never even conceive of such things, let alone duplicate them.

CHAPTER TWELVE

God's Commandments

When I wrote the title for this chapter, I thought this would be simple. Then as I sat staring at the blank page, it soon became more complex and much more confusing. We live in a world of rules and regulations. As I consider different religions, each has its own set of rules. Devout Jews for example, try each day to adhere to a long list of rules in the hope of being good enough to please God. When I look at Christianity, the variety of rules just seem to explode as each denomination has created its own rule-book.

I decided the solution was to get back to basics and focus on God's foundational Commandments. In the Old Testament, God led Moses to the top of Mount Sinai and gave His Commandments. They are recorded in Exodus 20:1-17, and in summary state:

1) I am the Lord Your God. You shall have no other gods before me.

115

2) You shall not make for yourself any idols.

3) You shall not misuse the name of the Lord Your God.

4) Remember the Sabbath by keeping it Holy.

5) Honor your father and your mother.

6) You shall not murder.

7) You shall not commit adultery.

8) You shall not steal.

9) You shall not give false testimony against your neighbor.

10) You shall not covet your neighbor's property.

At the time, Moses was leading thousands of people through the wilderness on a journey to the Promised Land. It must have been a fearful and stressful time for everyone and Moses had the task of keeping them focused on God and maintaining peace. This set of rules would surely have provided the basics for living as a community. In fact, in some respect, they still form the basis for community living today as many have become the rule of law.

In my own experience, although I was not raised in a Jewish or a Christian household, I was still aware of the ten commandments and if pressed could have listed most if not all of them. They were, in a sense, part of the fabric of life, as I was growing up.

Although it was not a conscious decision on my part or that of my parents, most of these commandments were the foundation of my upbringing. Like most of us, I was raised knowing it was wrong to kill, steal, commit adultery, blaspheme, lie about others, and covet what other people owned. These things to me, were just part of being an acceptable member of society, but they were also important to my own integrity as a person.

As I consider these commandments now, I am not sure where their importance lies. The rules of law held little influence over me, it was my personal integrity, which prohibited my law breaking. In terms of God's rules, on a conscious level at least, it was a non-issue because God was not a part of my life. However, one could make an argument that my integrity was subconsciously God's influence over me, I don't know.

Now I take the Old Testament Commandments as accepted. For the most part, my focus today as a committed Christian is on God's Commandments as portrayed through Jesus' teaching in the New Testament. In Mark 12:30-31, Jesus distilled God's commandments down to, "Love the Lord your God with all your heart and with all your soul and with all your mind and with all your strength. The second is this: Love your neighbor as yourself." Interestingly, if you follow these two commandments, you will automatically fulfill the ten commandments of the Old Testament.

I think most Christians view these two verses as: Love God and Love Your Neighbor. While I can see this and certainly applaud the fact that it recognizes a need to 'love your neighbor.' I view Jesus words a little differently, as: Love God, Self, and Others. I believe this provides an important balance. Obviously the first priority must be to love God. However, Jesus also said, "Love your neighbor as yourself." There are clearly two elements to this statement, which I think hold equal importance.

In today's society, many are focused only on self, to the detriment of all around us. As Christians, we are guided to 'love your neighbor,' which is not only beneficial to society as a whole, it is rewarding to the individual. However, I believe that in order to become the person God made each of us to be, we must love self. After all God made us and God does not do inferior work. I think it is true to say that in loving self, we are better able to love others. Therefore, loving God, self, and others, is really what Jesus was, and still is, calling us to do.

Once we accept the need to love God, self, and others, the next obvious question is - How? The short answer is, love is being in relationship. And again, the question is – How?

I believe being thankful to God is one way I can demonstrate my love for God. Each morning and evening I try to take a few moments to thank God for my previous night's sleep or for my day. I think about the good things that occurred over the last twelve hours. I may be thankful for peaceful restful sleep or thankful that it is morning after a restless night. I give thanks for the things I have done or seen, or the people I have talked to. Giving thanks and sharing thoughts are the beginning of a relationship with God. Then comes the hard part for me, to stop talking and listen.

If love is being in relationship, then how does one love self. The answer is to stop doing and spend time 'being,' in other words spend time with yourself. I was raised to believe I should be thinking about and taking care of others, with no consideration for myself. I did not give any time to thinking about myself. I was always busy doing things and my thoughts were only about 'following the rules.' I don't even think my steps in life were particularly thoughtful or conscious.

I just knew I was supposed to go to school; do my best; help my mother; carry out my chores; find a husband; get married; and become the person he wanted me to be.

Sadly, it was not until after my husband's death that I took the time to stop running around, keeping busy, and take the time 'to be.' In hindsight, part of it was fear of the silence, and only when I had found God was in the silence was it 'safe' for me to stop running. In fact, it was at this time I went into counseling because I realized that in order to know God, I needed to know me.

People today, particularly young people, are different, in that they appear to be focused almost exclusively on self. However, this seems to be from a materialistic perspective not a spiritual one. Life is about 'the world should revolve around what I want or need.' They do not necessarily spend time running around doing things, instead they are engaged in listening to music or digital communications. Their time, mind and energy seems to be completely consumed by electronic gadgets. However, it came as a surprise to me to realize we are still alike in the sense that we both fill our minds with noise and distractions, possibly they, too, are afraid of finding 'self' in the silence.

Self-centeredness is not love of self. It is not about getting to know who you are and certainly not, who God made you to be. Love for self is about who you are in God and this requires finding yourself in the silence. In this age of technology, I can only suggest that all of us need to regularly spend some time without the distraction of our electronic devices and listen to the silence. I submit that until you take some time to find yourself, you cannot love yourself.

119

In truth, God made each one of us. Each of us is precious in His sight. Even if you have not always lived a good life or always done the right things, I know from experience that trying to drown out life with noise will not change things. Maybe it is time to consider a different option and face your shortcomings. Accept them as past, embrace the future and learn to love yourself.

This brings us to Love Your Neighbor or 'love others.' Surprisingly, this completes a circle, in that making a commitment to love God; finding and loving self; I found naturally leads to loving others. At this point it becomes self-perpetuating as seeing joy in others, affects you and leads you to thank God.

In a regular home, we have neighbors living around us. They are usually people we come to know at some level, whether it is just acknowledging them when we go to the mailbox or spending time socializing with them on a regular basis. One way or another, we know who they are. At the same time, the church encourages an expansion of the 'neighbor' concept, to include people in the community who are in need.

Life in an RV brings a new perspective to 'Love Your Neighbor.' Based on the previous criteria, which revolves around a fixed neighborhood, it cannot happen. You are either moving around or the people around you are moving around. We traveled across the country over a period of five months, not staying anywhere for more than a few weeks. Then we arrived here in Florida and although we have stayed in one place for three months, the people around us have come and gone. We have met many people in the course of our journey, we have had brief encounters and in depth conversations.

Some people we have met, we will continue to keep in touch with, and others we will probably never see or talk to again.

So the question arises, what really constitutes loving one's neighbor. Of course, it does not mean rushing over and flinging your arms around everyone you meet in the street. Although, there are circumstances when such an action is both appropriate and desirable. I believe, loving one's neighbor is often just being present for someone, in whatever capacity they need it, whether you know there is a need or not. Just the simple act of taking the time to say a few kind words to someone, even a complete stranger, is an act of love.

While we were in Ohio, the owner of the campground suffered a life threatening medical event and spent several days in hospital. He did not have a staff to cover for his absence, but we witnessed friends and campers rally around to cover for him while he was away. This is clearly an example of showing love towards one's neighbor.

I believe each person we have met on our travels has been our neighbor in God's eyes. Some have been brought into our lives by God for our benefit, and I believe we were brought into the lives of others for their benefit. Remember we embarked on this journey based on zero knowledge of travel in an RV. In our travels, we have met people who have willingly shared invaluable advice in numerous different areas. One of the particular gifts of this lifestyle has been the interactions with people. Everyone it seems, wants to share their knowledge and experience to help others avoid the pitfalls they endured. Although many probably do not view it as such, this to me is the true meaning of love your neighbor.

On this journey I have discovered that following God's commandments, to the best of my ability, has changed me. As I have stated, I take a few moments each day to connect with God by giving thanks. I have also taken time to reflect and learn more about how to love myself. These two factors have given me a new sense of peace and joy, which manifests naturally in love for my neighbor. I have in the past, been a quiet introverted person and even before this journey began, I tended to talk to people only when necessary. This lifestyle has changed my perspective, and I find God prompts me to speak kindly to everyone I meet. When someone says something kind or helps me in a store, I frequently respond with 'Bless You,' and I know this comes from God, because it is not a natural response for me.

The unexpected 'side effect' of living in an attitude of thanksgiving is that it seems to be self-perpetuating. By this I mean, the more I speak to others in love, the better I feel about myself. As a result, I find that I rarely get angry or frustrated. Even when things do not go well, my negativity quickly subsides.

Nugget of Information:

First, to recognize and embrace all three aspects of Jesus' Commandment – to Love God; Self; and Others. Second, to appreciate that 'your neighbor,' is not geographically defined – our neighbor is everywhere. And third, thanksgiving becomes self-perpetuating.

CHAPTER THIRTEEN

Miracles

How does one define 'a miracle?' I used to think about a miracle as one of those momentous events in the Bible, which are beyond normal reason. Miracles were performed by Jesus, or His disciples, or in the Old Testament when God was guiding Moses as he led his people out of Egypt. I always perceived them as major events. I guess they had to be to have warranted being recorded in the Bible. In general, miracles were something that had occurred in the past, but not today.

When we started this journey across the country in our RV, I had to rethink my definition of a miracle. One thing in my mind did not change, I still believe miracles come from God. However, I have now come to understand them as events, large or small, which are beyond the norm of human interaction. They are events or situations, which defy logic and normal life expectations, as such they must be from

123

God. I am sure many people would brush them off as coincidence or accident, probably anxious to dismiss any possibility that God may have a hand in guiding His people today.

I have known from the beginning that our new adventure was prompted by God. It began when our friend told me how he had concluded his home had simply been a place to house the stuff he had collected and God showed me that the same was true for me. I knew, God was calling me to a changed life, although I did not understand its significance at the time. Although everything has physically changed, in that our home is on wheels and we move from place to place. The real change is, that I now rely more on God in all aspects of my life. I am completely outside my range of knowledge and we are away from the support of family and friends, our only constant is each other and God.

As our journey began, I quickly recognized the hand of God in the simple events of daily life. Things fell into place with a consistency beyond the realm of coincidence and left me with no choice other than to accept we were 'in God's hands.' As I acknowledged and embraced this, by giving thanks to God, the miracles just kept coming.

They range from simple things like guiding us to the Elks Club, which provided us with a safe haven in Newport when we made our very first trip, to ensuring we got back to the dealership to address issues before heading out across the country, to the truly miraculous.

My only regret was that on one occasion, I did not recognize the actual presence of God until after the event. I was alone, sitting on the sofa in the coach, and saw a light on the floor by the refrigerator.

I am, by nature, a practical person, who has always looked to science and logic for answers. I have little imagination and no experience with the unexplainable. The light was really bright and seemed to pulsate, my reaction was one of fear and not knowing what to do I prayed, but the light did not go away. I looked around for a logical answer and noticed a skylight where we have a fan. As the sun was shining, I reasoned the light on the floor was from the sun, so I put my hand over the skylight expecting to cast a shadow on the floor. Not only was there no shadow, there was no light shining on my hand, so the source could not have been from the skylight. As I continued to look at the pulsating light, it seemed to emanate from the floor, instead of reflecting onto the floor. I regret that I remained afraid until it finally faded and disappeared. It was only afterwards that I realized the light was from God and I had allowed my human fears to mask the miracle. I will always regret that I missed this opportunity, but I do know without any doubt, that God has blessed our RV home and travels with us.

In driving a big rig like ours, a thirty-seven foot coach plus a car towed behind it, the cardinal rule is never to enter a place without knowing you can get out. On one occasion we were on the road and I needed to take a bathroom break. We spotted a Flying J gas station, known to all RVers as a good place to stop as they are spacious to accommodate trucks. As I pulled in, I saw a sign for RVs and without thinking turned in. Too late, I realized it was for gas only and after pulling through the pump area, I was stranded in a small parking lot. I found a place to pull over and spotted a gate at the back of the lot, which would take me into the truck parking area, however, there was a truck blocking the way unloading fuel. I surveyed the area and determined this was my only way out, so I went in search of the tanker driver. He quickly advised me that he could not let me through as he was required to close the gate on leaving. I pointed to our rig, explained that I was a complete amateur and appealed to his good nature. He looked around, then nodded and told me he would move over when he had finished pumping to let me out. Once again, God came through for me, not only in the form of a kind truck driver, but also, in the fact the gate was open in the first place.

Every motor-home has some problems, even if it is new. We were able to address some issues before leaving Oregon and we knew we were headed in the direction of the factory to be able to correct future problems. While we were in Ohio, we were relatively close to the Newmar factory, but we knew that when we left for the winter, we would not have any fallback support system. It was, therefore, important to resolve any issues before heading to our winter location in Florida.

We had no idea what may arise, but once again God had us covered. While parked in Waynesville, Ohio, the house lights began to fail, one light at a time. I made a call to the factory and learned, there had been a recall by the lighting unit manufacturer and we could either get the failed ones fixed or have all of them switched out. We arranged to go back to the factory and get all of them switched out. However, before our appointment, when I took a shower, there was a loud creak below the shower floor and I found water leaking out on the floor from under the shower. In the next few weeks, we discovered a few other problems, so everything could be addressed at one time.

When we arrived at the factory, we were told that the lighting company had revised their policy and were only replacing fixtures that had failed. However, as we had been informed all would be changed, they would honor the arrangement. Then, as they addressed the shower issue, they found that the sub-structure under the shower unit had been incorrectly installed, leading to a substantial repair. This was not visible or obvious until the leak was identified, and would have been a major problem had we left the area without addressing it.

While at Newmar, the technician helped us to understand the precautions to be taken in the event of a cold and frosty night. This education proved to be very timely and invaluable as we subsequently experienced 28 degree nights before finally leaving Ohio.

In addition, to these experiences, there have been numerous occasions on our journey when God has led us to the right RV park and found us the right spot to park or the only spot left to park. He has guided us on the road through wind and rain. God has helped us find our way when the GPS failed us, due to road changes from road-work or just a bad road surface, which bounced the coach and we lost the signal.

We arrived in Carrabelle, Florida for the winter and although our traveling is on hold for a while, the miracles have not ceased. God brought us to a very quiet, backwater, in Florida and Barb was immediately concerned it would be too quiet. Although I am content at home, Barb needs the outside stimulus of people. God led us to a church here and through it brought us into the community. As a result, Barb has found contentment even in this small community. We have also found new friends here in the campground who come back year after year and reunite.

In addition to the unexpected friendships, God has taken particularly good care of us with regard to the weather. We have watched the news as major weather systems have moved across the country from the west, but have repeatedly dwindled to almost nothing before reaching here. We have looked at weather events that have occurred in areas we had considered before settling on this out of the way location and been thankful that God guided us to this place. The odd storm that has gone through this area has given us brief periods of heavy rain and some wind, but none of it has been damaging.

Taken individually, some of these events may be put down to luck. However, when viewed together and added to the many other experiences recorded in these pages, even the most cynical individual could not write them off as coincidence. The only possible conclusion to be drawn is the undeniable Hand of God.

The lessons I have learned with regard to miracles, is first that God is still making miracles happen. In fact, this whole book is a testimony to miraculous events. Second, it is up to us to expect miracles, look out for the miraculous and acknowledge miracles when they occur. I believe nothing makes God happier than to have His work recognized and to receive thanks for it. After all, isn't that what we all thrive on and we were made in God's image.

Nugget of Information:

Miracles are for the here and now, but each of us must both look for them and expect them.

CHAPTER FOURTEEN

Conclusion

The story of Jesus walking on water to catch up with the disciples in their boat and Peter stepping out of the boat to meet Jesus (Matt. 14:22-35), really 'struck home' with me in taking this journey. This may seem a little odd, because an RV on the road, is about as far as you can get from a boat in the water. However, like Peter, we had to get out of the boat!

I have spoken at length about putting ourselves in God's hands on this journey, but it started with 'getting out of the boat.' In the comfort and safety of our home in Oregon, I felt in control. In retrospect I realize this was an illusion, in truth, none of us are ever in control. However, I only came to understand this when we were driving down the road in a vehicle larger than I had ever imagined, and it finally dawned on me that everything I knew as normal no longer applied to my life. At that point I had two choices, either to retreat into a self-centered pity party of fear and doubt or celebrate the freedom and adventure, in the belief that God brought us here and He will take care of us. Granted our situation was a little extreme, but in reality, all of us make those choices every day. So, the first lesson I learned was – get out of the boat!

The second lesson is determining the direction God has set for you. In our case, the whole process took a couple of years. God has a plan for each one of us and it may take time. Ask God for direction, then listen for His direction. If you have options, ask God for guidance, but remember the right one may not have been revealed yet, so in praying for guidance always provide God with 'a none of the above' option.

Third, when you have received direction from God, two factors must drive your way forward. It begins with faith, which is trusting in God and having thoughts and emotions consistent with the Word of God. The second factor, which is often unrecognized is Belief. This is more easily explained through the term Unbelief, which means thoughts, emotions and actions opposed to God's Word. In other words, unbelief is the opposite of faith and as such can negate the power of Faith. If you ask God for guidance and begin your journey in faith, then allow negative thoughts and doubts to invade your mind, unbelief sets in, and failure follows.

This was and is an ongoing challenge for me. I have spent most of my life functioning only on the understanding that we have five senses – what we can touch, smell, hear, taste, and see. These are the senses of the carnal world and as such are the devil's dominion. On this journey, I am learning about my sixth sense, which is recognized only through the spirit realm and therefore beyond Satan's influence.

It is a sense of 'knowing' that comes from within oneself without any logical explanation. This is 'activated' through the Word of God and through it I am developing a relationship with God. I have found that studying the Word of God is reprogramming my mind to keep my thoughts positive. For example, in the past, I have focused on potential problems, and expended my energy in trying to figure out appropriate responses for every scenario. Nowadays, I recognize that I am not in control of my life and never have been. Instead of trying to plan for every eventuality, I turn to God for guidance and believe He will take care of it, whatever the outcome.

Believing I am in God's hands and as a result whatever happens will be where He wants me to be, has given me a sense of peace not previously experienced. On our journey, we have often had plans, but always with an element of flexibility in them. I guess I still like to think I have control sometimes, but I have come to a place where I accept that I do not have all the answers – and that's okay!

My new understanding of God and my relationship with God has turned some of the religious conventions, I had previously learned, on their head. In the past, one of my consistent prayers has been to 'Ask God to be with me.' In studying the Word of God, I read Matt. 28:20 in which Jesus says "And surely, I am with you always, to the very end of the age." On this basis, asking God to be with me, is expressing doubt and unbelief. In the same way, we tend to ask God to do things for us, but in truth, Jesus told us that we have been given those powers in His name. Therefore, to ask God to do things for us that have already been done by Jesus sacrifice on the cross is, at best, unbelief. The solution is to stop asking God for what we already have and take the authority He has given us – pray to manifest what we need in the name of Jesus Christ.

One of the main things I have learned is how much influence my thoughts and words have both on me, and on those around me. Prov. 18:21 - "Death and life are in the power of the tongue." And Prov. 23:7 – "As he thinks, so is he." These two proverbs speak directly to this subject. If you take them to heart as I have done, you will completely change your thinking. It gives you a whole new perspective on the things you allow to enter your mind, especially when you consider the bombardment of negativity from the media. I still listen to some news and some programs with negative content, but I am more conscious of them and try to counter them by including more positive input in my life.

As far as my thoughts are concerned, with respect to negative thoughts, I try to keep in mind the phrase – do not conceive things, you do not want to birth. In other words, I try to keep positive thoughts. However bad your day may have been, remember, it is an awesome day, because God loves you!

AND FINALLY.........

I began this book with the question, 'where do you look for God?' Then I answered it by saying. "Most recently I found God in an RV." In the chapters that followed, I have tried to show you my experiences of finding God as we traveled.

However, what has become clear to me in writing this book, is that I did not really look for God at all. When we started our journey, I already knew that God was a part of me, although from my perspective at least, He was 'a dormant partner.' In the business of living, my relationship with God had been limited to a few minutes a day, most days. I had other things to do, so I gave God a low priority.

When Barb and I embarked on a whole new journey into the unknown, I placed a new priority level on my relationship with God. As a result, I did not find God, He found me!

I committed more consistent time each day to studying God's Word. As a result, although it was not a particularly conscious effort, my thoughts more consistently turned to God. As we traveled across the country and saw the beauty it displays each and every day, it seemed only natural to recognize God at work. In the small details of our journey, like discovering a problem with the towing system while in Newport and close to the dealership where we could get it fixed, instead of having the problem after we left the state, I knew God was taking care of us.

We started the journey believing it was at God's direction and as each day passed, it became more clear that He was prompting, guiding and protecting us in all aspects of our travels. In truth, this adventure was completely outside the realm of anything I had ever done and as such, would have been impossible under my own ability. I think both Barb and I knew we needed God, if we were to stand any chance of success, as the list of unknown factors and new things to learn was seemingly endless.

However, as this book attests, God's role was and continues to be the guiding factor. He has helped us in time of need; shown us wonders of nature beyond our imagination; given us unique gifts like our bison encounters; protected us from potential disasters, like providing instruction in the event of freezing weather only a couple of weeks before we found ourselves unexpectedly in below freezing weather; and finding us a safe haven in Florida while providing us with a much needed sense of community.

I have always been proud of my ability to make meticulous plans, to cover every eventuality. However, I have to concede that God has proven Himself to be much better at organizing our lives, than I could ever have done.

The lesson, I believe, is to realize that God is to be found wherever you are, because He is already within you. All you need to do is reach out to Him through His Word. This is the beginning of spending time with God and the start of a relationship with God. As the relationship develops, your focus shifts more towards God and away from the distractions of life. I hope that this story will inspire you to begin to look for and see God at work in your life, not necessarily in big events, but in the small details.

I know my perspective has shifted and I now look at setbacks or delays in our journey as gifts, choosing to believe that God has protected us from some unseen problem. Of course, I may never know what they may have been. However, when we were delayed in traveling to the Elks in Keizer, Oregon and encountered traffic delays due to an earlier accident, both of us wondered if God had saved us from being a part of the accident. I know only that God has the full picture and I barely constitute a speck in the whole scheme of things.

I have always been a person who needed to be in control. This journey has taught me that trusting in God instead of myself, and my ability to plan for every eventuality, is freeing. There is much less stress in knowing that whatever happens, we are in God's hands. When we travel, we prayerfully plan and have a destination for the night, then trust God will take care of it, even if there are delays.

When we decided to embark on this adventure, we knew it was beyond our ability to control the results, so in a sense, we had no choice but to trust God. In many ways this situation was easier than trusting God in the everyday events of life. I know from my own experience, that at intervals throughout my life, I have turned over control to God, only to take it back when I thought it was not going the right way or fast enough. It has been much easier to stay in God's hands now that I don't know where I am going and have even less idea of how to get there.

In this journey, I have concluded from everything I have learned, that walking in a relationship with God is simple, but it is not easy. However, it is most definitely worth it. All I can suggest to you, is to place yourself in God's hands without any preconceived idea of the result. It seems to me, to be the only way to resist any temptation to 'critique God,' and take back control.

I thank God for the journey He is now leading me on and I wish you Godspeed and God's Blessings in your journey!

70256132R00076

Made in the USA
Columbia, SC
06 May 2017